D0170813

THE WORLD OF JAMES BOND

THE WORLD OF JAMES BOND

The Lives and Times of 007

Jeremy Black

ROWMAN & LITTLEFIELD
Lanham • Boulder • New York • London

Published by Rowman & Littlefield
A wholly owned subsidiary of
The Rowman & Littlefield Publishing Group, Inc.
4501 Forbes Boulevard, Suite 200, Lanham, Maryland 20706
https://rowman.com

Unit A, Whitacre Mews, 26-34 Stannary Street, London SE11 4AB,
United Kingdom

Copyright © 2017 by Rowman & Littlefield

All rights reserved. No part of this book may be reproduced in any form or by
any electronic or mechanical means, including information storage and retriev-
al systems, without written permission from the publisher, except by a reviewer
who may quote passages in a review.

British Library Cataloguing in Publication Information Available

Library of Congress Cataloging-in-Publication Data
Names: Black, Jeremy M., 1955– author.
Title: The world of James Bond / Jeremy Black.
Description: Lanham : Rowman & Littlefield, 2017. | Includes index.
Identifiers: LCCN 2017011420 (print) | LCCN 2017027136 (ebook) | ISBN
   9781442276123 (electronic) | ISBN 9781442276116 (cloth : alk. paper)
Subjects: LCSH: James Bond films—History and criticism. | Fleming, Ian,
   1908–1964—Characters—James Bond. | Bond, James (Fictitious character)
Classification: LCC PN1995.9.J3 (ebook) | LCC PN1995.9.J3 B53 2017 (print)
   | DDC 791.43/75—dc23
LC record available at https://lccn.loc.gov/2017011420

∞ ™ The paper used in this publication meets the minimum requirements of
American National Standard for Information Sciences Permanence of Paper
for Printed Library Materials, ANSI/NISO Z39.48-1992.

Printed in the United States of America

For Greg Clark

CONTENTS

PREFACE

Fictional characters take on the world. Let us start with one of the greatest, and not, for the moment, James Bond. He will stride in soon enough. In the mid-twentieth century, Sherlock Holmes, a consummate puzzle solver and small-scale adventure hero, was translated afresh to the screen by a revolver-armed Basil Rathbone. The corpus was brought up to date as, from 1938 to 1946, Holmes, still in deerstalker, was taken from the London streets to new destinations—Canada, the United States, and Algiers—and given contemporary concerns and foes, in particular, but not only, the Nazis. In *Sherlock Holmes and the Voice of Terror* (1942), the best of this film series and one that uses elements from the Conan Doyle story "His Last Bow," Holmes is on home ground and thwarts a Nazi program of sabotage and an attempted German invasion whose mastermind is none other than the head of the British Intelligence Coordination Committee, Sir Evan Barham.

As a reminder of the usual rule of detective fiction—that the detective intervenes to restore a harmony disrupted by the hubristic evil of crime—Barham is not really the Home Counties gent he appears to be, but a German agent who took his place when the real Barham was shot by the Germans in cold blood while a prisoner in World War I. Like most fictional villains, Barham is also overconfident; he brings Holmes into the case to appear to be doing everything possible to thwart the Nazis. There are many echoes of Barham in the presentation of Drax, really a Nazi, in Ian Fleming's *Moonraker* (1955), while the overconfidence of the villains is part of the heady mix of intrigue, suspense, and adventure that makes a Fleming novel. In 1963, in a letter to Fleming, the British poet John Betjeman compared Bond to an international Holmes.

As with Bond, Holmes richly repays a treatment that updates his setting and is best understood in terms of these changing settings. In Conan Doyle's hands, he changed, eventually, in response to the pressure of events in the early twentieth century, thwarting German invasion plans. Other writers subsequently recast Holmes, for example, to include a married Holmes, and he has been extensively interpreted on television and in film, not least with greater interest in his drug addiction.

The same process of reinterpretation is true of Agatha Christie's Hercule Poirot and Ian Fleming's James Bond. Poirot, a figure of Fleming's youth and adulthood who went on appearing regularly in new adventures after Fleming's early death in 1964, might seem to be a timeless figure. However, in practice, Poirot recorded shifting political concerns and assumptions, as well as the details of daily life, such as the role of servants. In the post–World War II *At Bertram's Hotel* (1965), Christie noted that the opulence of the interwar years had gone, and that the echo of it must be a sign of a criminal organization: "the headquarters of one of the best and biggest crime syndicates that's been known for years."

Earlier, in a number of interwar novels, Christie recorded the standard fears of affluent British society in adventure stories, spicing them with the paranoid conviction of an underlying conspiracy. This was not a case of the isolated murderer. In *The Big Four* (1927), one of her least-known novels, but one that is significant politically and redolent of wider themes in British culture and society, Christie told readers near the outset about

> The world-wide unrest, the labour troubles that beset every nation, and the revolutions that break out in some. . . . There is a force behind the scenes which aims at nothing less than the disintegration of civilization. . . . Lenin and Trotsky were mere puppets.

This idea of a secret conspiracy behind everything was also central to the Bond novels and films. The 1927 conspiracy was wide ranging in its goals and means: Christie presented technology as at the service of this force; the "Big Four" sought "a concentration of wireless energy far beyond anything so far attempted, and capable of focusing a beam of great intensity upon some given spot" and also "atomic energy," such that they could become "the dictators of the world."

Poirot thwarted the "Big Four" in a Bond-like finale in Switzerland; but, in contrast, he usually relied on using his "little grey cells" rather than force, and certainly not deadly force. This was not a one-off. Christie returned to the theme of global conspiracies in *Passenger to Frankfurt* (1970), which warns of "The Ring," a global network that moves armaments, including germ warfare weapons, to anarchist forces that overlap with neo-Nazis and "Youth Power." This sort of stuff does not make Fleming appear too extraordinary. Instead, this strong theme, which ranged across several literary genres, both fictional and factual, in Britain, the United States, and elsewhere, prepared readers for Bond stories.

In contrast both to Poirot and to many adventure stories, Bond both solves the puzzle and repeatedly uses deadly force, indeed in the films force on an industrial scale. He is the most successful adventure hero in history, thwarting "the instruments of Armageddon" in the film *The Spy Who Loved Me* (1977), saving the world as the seconds tick away in *Moonraker* (1979, the film, not the novel), and holding off the destruction of world agriculture in *On Her Majesty's Secret Service* (1969) or nuclear war in *You Only Live Twice* (1967). Other victims saved on different occasions more modestly include London: novel *Moonraker* (1955); American rocketry: *Dr. No* (novel and film); Miami: film *Thunderball* (1965); Washington: film *Diamonds Are Forever* (1971); and so on. The enormity of the villains' ambitions help to make Bond a relevant figure for an age first of apocalyptic nuclear scenarios and, subsequently, one of terrorist threats, which were a characteristic not only of the 2000s and 2010s, but also of the 1970s.

There is extensive literature on Bond, though most of it is of the exploitation type and makes scant attempt to consider adequately Bond's context and the change in the plots and character. The most distinguished discussant, the Italian structuralist academic Umberto Eco, writing in the 1960s about the novels, presented Bond in terms of the creation of a recognizable and potent type through the use of consistent narrative structure, although the comparisons with mythic status in the operas of Wagner might surprise some readers, and were arresting rather than helpful. Moreover, his was a short work.

In practice, Bond provides a fascinating source for changing views about the world. This is true of the narratives of the Fleming books, of the films, and of the many books involving Bond published by others after Fleming died at age fifty-six in 1964—books that are generally neglected. Both novels and films drew on current fears to reduce the implausibility of the villains and their villainy. The novels and films also presented potent images of national character, explored the rapidly changing relationship between a declining Britain and an ascendant United States, charted the course of the Cold War and of the subsequent new postwar (post-1990) world, and offered a changing but potent demonology. Bond was, and still is, an important aspect of post–World War

II (post-1945) popular culture, not only in Britain but more generally. This was particularly so after the Americans financed the filmic Bond, thus making him a character designed for the world's greatest film market, but also a world product and, linked to this, a figure of globalization.

Class, place, gender, violence, sex, race—all are themes that can be scrutinized through the shifts in characterization and plot. So also can be both popular culture and the relationship between fiction and fact. In the BBC Radio 4 program "The Politics of James Bond," broadcast on January 1, 2001, that I planned and narrated, the interview with Oleg Gordievsky was the item that excited most press comment. He was head of the KGB station in Copenhagen and London, as well as an agent for the British who eventually defected in 1985. Gordievsky claimed that the Central Committee of the Soviet Communist Party watched Bond films, that they accordingly instructed him to secure a copy as soon as a new one came out, and that the KGB also asked him to obtain the devices Bond used so that they could ascertain their viability.

More significantly, Gordievsky suggested that the Bond stories contributed to the reputation of British intelligence, which serious Soviet penetration had greatly compromised in the 1940s and 1950s. Such comments are a reminder that popular culture is not a distinct subject, widely separated from the real world of politics, but, instead, a factor that helps to shape the latter just as the latter shapes it. If only for that reason, the politics and world of Bond rest in large part on the perceptions of those who read and/or watched the stories.

This book offers a historian's "take" on Bond from the perspective of the late 2010s, and the issues and questions of the period. In particular, I assess Bond in terms of the greatly changing world order of the Bond years, a lifetime that stretches from 1953 to the present. This changing world order is one of the relative decline of Britain and the dominance of the United States, including in the cultural sphere, and especially after the collapse of the Communist Bloc in 1989–1991. The focus will be on the Fleming novels and the Eon films, but there will also be consideration of later, non-Fleming, novels and of films using Bond that were not part of the official sequence. Bond's role in world culture has become even greater as he has acquired a quasi-hereditary status, with the children and grandchildren of original audiences now watching.

In 2001, when the Fleming novels were out of print in the United States, I published *The Politics of James Bond*, a book written in 1999 that covered the subject up until then, in both the novels and films. I did not seek to write a second edition, based on revising that book. However, the Bond world has both continued and changed and, in response, I have also given many lectures on the subject. With the arrival of a new M in 2015 and the subsequent drawing toward a close of the Daniel Craig era, it is time to think of an entirely new book. This is not least because the Cold War and Britain as a great power are both recognizably long departed. If Russia wishes to restart the Cold War, as was frequently claimed in the mid-2010s, it is a different one to that which ended in 1989. The gender and social politics of the original Bond have also largely gone, although the world of Bond has now lasted longer than that of most readers and film watchers. The cultural context for Bond now is very different, including the rise of the Jason Bourne films based on the Robert Ludlum character.

I owe a great debt to those who have allowed me to develop my thoughts by inviting me to give lectures and to the many conversations and extensive correspondence I have had accordingly. I am especially grateful for invitations to speak at the Bond conference at the University of Indiana in 2003; to the Great Lives Series at Mary Washington University; at the College of William and Mary; the Universities of Cincinnati, Exeter, North

Carolina–Asheville, North Georgia, Ohio, Rheims, Southeastern Louisiana, and Washington; Appalachian State, Assumption, Auburn, and George Washington universities; Keble College, Oxford; the New Jersey Institute of Technology; the Foreign Policy Research Institute in Philadelphia; the New York Military Affairs Symposium; Eastern Nazarene College; the Budleigh Salterton Literary Festival; the Exeter University History Society; the Exeter Medical Society; Torquay Museum; Williamsburg Public Library; Wellington College; Stowe School; to the annual conference of the Chartered Institute of Payroll Professionals; the Devon Cambridge Society; for three meetings Norton Rose arranged; and on a number of radio programs, American, British, and Irish. I have also enjoyed lecturing on Bond on liners in the Caribbean, Pacific, Atlantic, North Sea, and Mediterranean, and on boats on the Danube, Rhine, and Rhone.

I have benefited from the editorial advice of Susan McEachern, from the comments on an earlier draft of Steve Bodger, Stan Carpenter, Keith Laybourn, Ryan Patterson, and Heiko Werner Henning, and from the comments of Joyce Goffin, Marc Palen, and Stephen Perring on particular chapters. I dedicate this book to Greg Clark, a friend who shares my interest in Bond.

I

POLITICAL BACKGROUND

First presented in the novel *Casino Royale* in 1953, when Britain was still a great imperial power, James Bond has been the killing arm of the British state through decades of transformation. He has been both unchanging, a man of great determination, energy, fortitude, and success, and yet obliged to respond to these transformations. That contrast provides the dynamic of this book, the history of the secret agent as adventure hero while the world changed. The move from novel to film was a key transition for Bond, but not the only one that explains his success. The ability to move from a 1950s British specificity, a Bond who made sense largely in British terms and to British readers, to a more generalized political setting has also been crucial to the conceptual, as well as commercial, success of Bond, providing global appeal and lasting resonances for the character and his adventures. At the same time, Bond's specific Britishness may be a part of his success, even for foreign readers and film viewers, this being a characteristic he shares with Sherlock Holmes, just as the characterization and role of Hercule Poirot depends on his being a foreigner in Britain.

It is by no means easy to explain success; the reasons that people choose to read particular books, or to see and enjoy specific films and not others, vary greatly. Furthermore, even at the individual level, more than one factor may play a role in explaining preferences. Moreover, this is even more the case when addressing the past; market research was less developed then. In addition, processes of change are relatively easy to record, chart, and apparently explain, at least in the sense of argument by means of assertion, but in practice the situation is different insofar as offering a fine analysis of cause and effect is concerned. After all, consumers, us in short, are both individuals and members of groups. It is all too easy to treat them as the latter and thus to offer abstractions, whether on national, gender, class, age, sexuality, or on other grounds, to explain group and individual choices, as is done with market research. These abstractions certainly can be valuable, and they need to be probed. However, such abstractions also serve to reify and explain processes that are inherently complex and more varied. These points need to be borne in mind in everything that follows.

Bond was very much a Cold War figure when launched, and was presented and seen in those terms. Indeed, he was a new version of the interwar British "Clubland heroes," those gentlemen heroes who were brave and decent chaps, such as Sapper's resolute creation "Bulldog" Drummond. Sapper was the pseudonym of Herman C. McNeile (1888–1937), a soldier turned novelist who created Hugh "Bulldog" Drummond, a patriotic defender, in a series of ten novels, four short stories, four stage plays, and a screenplay from 1920 to 1937, of all that was right against a flock of villains, mostly foreign. His friend Gerard Fairlie continued the stories between 1938 and 1954, with others following in the 1960s and one in 1983. Bond was also an exemplar of these heroes and their fictionalized and (lest it be forgotten) very real World War II counterparts, for the more dour postwar Cold War. That application inherently posed challenges; the Cold War lacked the battlefield heroism and bravery, the adventure and the clarity, of World War II.

The latter was an experience that was very much present to Fleming's readers. They had fought in the war or, as civilians, experienced it at one remove, being bombed or evacuated, neither of which was true of American readers. Fleming referred to this experience in *Moonraker* (1955), the third Bond novel, when Winston Churchill as prime minister, as he indeed was again in 1951–1955, broadcasts to the nation on the value of the rocket project. Undercover Special Branch officer Gala Brand reflects that his is "the voice of all the great occasions in her life," which identifies the war, and notably fighting on with fortitude when defeated by Germany in 1940, as the key memory of her life— one that joins her wartime endurance to her postwar bravery.

Britain was actually at war when Fleming finished writing his first Bond novel in 1952. The war in question was the Korean War, which had begun in 1950 and continued into 1953. The Soviet- and Chinese-supported Communist North Koreans had launched an invasion of South Korea. In late 1950, changing the flow of the campaigning, large numbers of Chinese troops were added to the North Korean forces who were already backed by Soviet aircraft. In this conflict, Britain provided the UN-sanctioned force with the second-largest international contingent after the Americans, an element that tends to be forgotten or ignored. Alongside troops, ships and aircraft were sent, and the British were heavily involved. This was a Britain of conscription—one in which all men of a certain age could be expected to fight and to risk death. Their families had to accept this risk.

The Korean War, however, was not Bond's beat. The Bond of the novels was not to go to Korea and, indeed, only went to Japan in eventual pursuit of Blofeld, the head of SPECTRE, in *You Only Live Twice* (1964). Blofeld points out to Bond that British agents should not be in Japan. So also with the filmic Bond, who went to Japan for the film version of that title, but only went to Korea (North Korea in this case) once, in an inherently implausible adventure in *Die Another Day* (2002), which was late in the film corpus.

In the case of Fleming's geography, there was an inherent conservatism to his focus in the Cold War. Fleming's attention centered on what he knew—Europe, North America, and the West Indies—with the last linked to both Britain and the United States. In practice, the Cold War was very "hot" in East Asia between 1946 and 1954, and notably in China, Vietnam, Korea, and Malaya. Moreover, this pattern was to revive from the late 1950s with conflict in Laos, Vietnam, and Cambodia, that continued throughout Fleming's life, remaining large-scale until the late 1970s.

In addition, Britain was involved regionally, confronting Chinese-backed Communism in Malaya in the 1950s and Indonesian expansionism in northern Borneo in 1962–1966, the latter in the so-called Confrontation. The Indonesian government was nationalist, not Communist, but was increasingly linked to the Communist powers. Fleming, however, showed only limited interest in East Asia, with the exception of Japan and Macao, both of which he had visited, and somewhat unusually so for a Briton of his age. He visited Kuwait in 1960, being commissioned by the Kuwait Oil Company to write *State of Excitement* about the country, but did not enjoy his stay, finding the country dirty, and the company refused to publish the less-than-eulogistic book. Fleming was even less interested in South Asia.

Fleming's Cold War, that outlined for Bond, was different to that in Asia. This focus reflected the role of personal experience in his writing and the extent to which his imagination did not focus on what he had not known. Empire was a key theme for Fleming, but the coining of his experience, his experience conflated with his fantasy, was the vital means. This was true in every sense.

Fleming was born on May 28, 1908, into a wealthy and well-connected banking family, the second son of Valentine Fleming (1882–1917). His father was a landowner who would be killed on the western front in World War I. At the time of his death, Valentine was a Conservative MP; Churchill wrote the obituary for the *Times*. Fleming was educated at Eton, where he won the athletic prize two years running, and then at the Royal Military College, Sandhurst. Fleming, however, did not go into the army; he left Sandhurst without a commission in 1927. He did not appreciate army discipline and hours, did not like the mechanization of the army, and had contracted venereal disease. Fleming then spent time in Austria, being educated at a finishing school in Kitzbühel run by the former head of MI6 in Vienna, and at the universities of Munich and Geneva, but failed the examination to enter the Foreign Office, a key rite of passage for many in the elite. Nor did he enter politics as his father had done.

Instead, Fleming became a journalist, working for Reuters, the news agency, notably in Moscow in 1933 covering the trial of Allan Monkhouse, a British engineer accused of espionage. This was a posting that subsequently attracted attention as Fleming acted as an agent for MI6 then. From 1933, Fleming followed the family tradition, trying to earn money in finance, first in banking and then in stockbroking, but he did not enjoy it. However, that was not the point; these jobs provided an income to support social status and to pursue his hobbies, including high-stakes bridge, eating well, and collecting first editions of works seen as milestones of progress.

As for many men of his generation who survived, World War II "made" him. Fleming became the personal assistant to Admiral John Godfrey, the director of Naval Intelligence, and proved a success at the job, liaising with the other secret services, playing a role in clandestine operations, and being promoted to Commander. Working on intelligence cooperation with the United States before Pearl Harbor, Fleming visited Washington in 1941. To the same end, in 1942, he traveled to Jamaica for a naval conference with the United States. Fleming was posted to Spain in 1941–1942, and his visit to the Estoril casino in Portugal in 1941 probably provided inspiration for *Casino Royale*.

In writing his many memos, Fleming gained skill as a wordsmith. He also developed an interest in espionage history. Indeed, in 1953, Fleming was to tell Leonard Mosley, who also worked at the *Sunday Times*, that he had read during the war in the archives about the exploits of the secret agent Sidney Reilly, who had played a role in an unsuccessful 1918 British plot to overthrow Lenin, and would be assassinated by Soviet agents in 1925. Like Bond, Reilly was an enthusiastic gambler, liked the high life, and was keen on women. In the latter stage of the war, Fleming's role diminished, partly possibly because he did not get on well with Godfrey's successor, the somewhat bureaucratic Edmund Rushbrooke. Intelligence operations also involved Fleming's contacts. One close friend, Ivan Bryce, worked for the British Security Coordinator in New York.

In 1945, after demobilization, Fleming became foreign manager for the Kemsley newspaper group, which owned the *Sunday Times*. Fleming had met Lord Kemsley during his wartime work on press liaison. In this job, Fleming was in charge of its foreign correspondents at a time when British secret service agents were sometimes placed by such means. Fleming's contract allowed him three months' holiday every winter, which gave him time to write and to enjoy Goldeneye, the property he had bought on the northern shore of Jamaica in 1947 for £2,000. Marriage too spurred him to write. The sophisticated and well-connected Ann Charteris (1913–1981), his longtime mistress and a war widow, had a daughter, Mary, by Fleming in 1948, but Mary died shortly after birth. In 1951, Ann's second husband, Esmond, Second Viscount Rothermere, divorced her and she married Fleming in Jamaica in March 1952 before their only child, Caspar, was born that August.

The first novel, the rapidly written *Casino Royale* (1953), was particularly grounded in Fleming's knowledge of espionage and the relevant tradecraft (and in the novel's commitment to the dramatic unities of time, place, and action), while also representing a continuation of the interwar Clubland style, notably in the detailed discussion of the gambling. The latter was also seen in the extensive discussion of the fictional London club Blades in *Moonraker* (1955), the third novel, a discussion that drew on his own membership of Whites, Boodles, and the Portland Club, all distinguished clubs, and the last particularly significant for gambling. *Casino Royale* had the interest of a Continental setting, while the female lead, Vesper Lynd, was strong and, thanks to her, there was a puzzle to the close, which was not the case with *Moonraker*.

In some respects, *Casino Royale* and *Moonraker* were the "happiest" pieces of writing in the Bond corpus. They were both set in a Cold War in which the aftermath of World War II played a major role. Each novel presented the Soviet Union as an active force and one made more deadly by the support of agents within: Communist trade unionists in the first case and a disguised secret conspiracy in the second. *Casino Royale* has an immediacy that reflects Fleming's journalistic skills. The inscription in his own copy of the book kept with his papers noted:

> This was written in January and February 1952, accepted by Capes in the spring, and published a year later. It was written to take my mind off other matters at Goldeneye, Jamaica. The characters are not based on people but some of the incidents are factual. The bomb trick was used by the Russians in an attempt on Von Papen during the war in Ankara.

The here-and-now was important to the novels. At the end of *Moonraker*, M reflected that Britain had not come out of the Moonraker affair too badly:

> We've wanted one of their [Soviet] high-speed U-boats and we'll be glad of the clues we can pick up about their atom bombs. The Russians know that we know that their gamble failed. Malenkov's none too firmly in the saddle and this may mean another Kremlin revolt. As for the Germans. Well, we all knew there was plenty of Nazism left and this will make the Cabinet go just a bit more carefully on German rearmament.

In practice, West Germany was rearmed from 1955 as a member of NATO, with Britain not playing the key role in the matter. At least West Germany did not pursue nuclear capability, and its hopes of doing so were forestalled by the Americans maintaining control. The description of the rocket in the novel revealed Fleming's engagement with technology. Moreover, his knowledge of cars, routes, and driving, and notably of driving in the county of Kent, where he had a house in St. Margaret's Bay, was to the fore in the novel.

In contrast to these novels, wanderlust and a broader geographical and political scope were present from the second novel, *Live and Let Die* (1954), a novel written in early 1953 before Fleming had seen the reviews of *Casino Royale*. The new book sent Bond to help defend the United States against a Soviet-organized network of African Americans. If the Bond novels represented an instance of the "New Elizabethan Age" that supposedly accompanied the ascension of Elizabeth II in 1952 and her coronation in 1953, echoing the glories of the reign of Elizabeth I (1558–1603), then this story was very much a geographical expression of it that was not confined to empire nor indeed to Britain or to Western Europe. One of the victorious powers in World War II, this was a Britain that, despite parting with India and Pakistan in 1947, still had the largest empire in the world, notably in Africa, Southeast Asia, the West Indies, and the Pacific, as well as the second largest navy after the United States. It was the third nuclear power after the United States and the Soviet Union; it appeared to be charting a successful course to a modernity that was not divorced from tradition. This was the Britain of nuclear power stations and diesel trains (instead of the old steam trains), the Britain that, as Bond noted when standing up for the country against criticism in *You Only Live Twice* (1964), sent the team that, in 1953, first climbed Mt. Everest, the world's highest peak. Climbing was a sport that was regarded by many as being for gentlemen.

The geographical span of the Bond novels underlines the difficulties of classifying their politics as a whole. In part, they are novels in which empire is a theme, notably *Dr. No* (1958) or the brief Sierra Leone close of *Diamonds Are Forever* (1956), a novel largely set in the United States. This was an ending missing in the 1971 film, when Britain, after Sierra Leone's independence in 1961, was no longer the colonial power there. The focus on the British West Indies, as in *Live and Let Die* and *Thunderball*, reflected Fleming's life in Jamaica and his fascination with Caribbean waters and their marine life. This is seen in many descriptions. Thus, in *Thunderball*, Fleming writes of the villains:

> They swam on in the soft moonlit mist of the sea. At first there was nothing but a milky void below them, but then the coral shelf of the island showed up, climbing steeply towards the surface. Sea fans, like small shrouds in the moonlight, waved softly, beckoning, and the clumps and trees of coral were grey and enigmatic.

In addition, the genesis of *Dr. No* arose from a film treatment produced for an abortive attempt to persuade the British colonial government of Jamaica to make films for American television. The rest of Fleming's life was lived largely in southeast England, but he had seen much of Europe prewar. That helped ensure a

European focus in his account of the Cold War, and notably so with *Casino Royale*, with *From Russia, With Love*, and with the short stories "From a View to a Kill" (1960) and "The Living Daylights" (1962), as well as the European setting of *On Her Majesty's Secret Service* (1963).

At every turn, Fleming tried to make Britain's position a plot enabler and, at least to that extent, interesting to the reader. Thus, confrontation and struggle are in part a matter of the setting. Yet, in offering interest primarily to British readers, there was also a wider resonance, notably so in the treatment of the United States and the West Indies, and, more generally, in plot lines that threatened the United States. Although Fleming's prejudiced comments on deracination and Italian Americans in *Diamonds Are Forever* were ill advised, there was no anti-Americanism, certainly not to the extent of some of the "late-imperialist" British writers.

Indeed, Fleming was to enjoy a powerful moment of American popularity in the early 1960s, specifically thanks to the sponsorship of President John F. Kennedy and, very differently, Hugh Hefner. Fleming stayed at the White House and his short stories appeared in Hefner's *Playboy*, then an iconic magazine, and one that Bond is seen reading in the film *On Her Majesty's Secret Service* (1969), in a scene that now greatly jars. He is presented as a member of the Playboy Club in *Diamonds Are Forever* (1971). Fleming, and therefore Bond, became a key aspect of the Anglo-Americanism that was so important to the contours of Cold War culture in the late 1950s; it moved in the United States beyond the earlier, cruder anti-Communism. This was a transition already made in Britain.

Fleming had sought an Anglo-American role because he wanted to make his novels attractive to Hollywood, and the wealth and glamor it apparently offered, both of which his wife and lifestyle made necessary. Moreover, Hollywood's wealth and glamor were highlighted by the austerity and high taxation of Britain. Indeed, the search for Hollywood was not only an aspect of the dominance of America, and of Fleming's understanding of how the world had moved from the British Empire of the 1930s, but also crucial to the development of Bond. The alternative, a British film version, as briefly seemed possible after an approach from the producer Sir Alexander Korda in 1953, would have been far less potent on the global scale. This was the case both for commercial reasons and because such a character would probably have been confined to a more conservative location in the class system at a stage in which this system was fragile and fast changing.

Hollywood meant, and made, a global brand and ambition, the two mutually dependent. This goal and means forced adjustments, or, rather, a transformation. There would have been a change had the medium of Bond remained the novel, a possibility that invites consideration. However, the medium change was to film, and in a predominantly American context. The global brand was somewhat problematic in this case; it was necessary to make a British agent and his world viable, in an American-type and American-distributed film series, to a global, although principally American, audience.

This transformation provided opportunities, as well as posed problems. The opportunities included the interaction, at times contrast, between cultures, which helped explain the importance of the Felix Leiter character, the CIA agent who proves Bond's helpful collaborator, playing a supportive, but secondary, role. The beginning of the film *Dr. No* (1962) captured the theme of national identification with the scene of Big Ben, an iconic London location, and then the setting of an episode and the introduction of Bond in a then classic British casino. This casino itself was a major contrast to the American-style casino later seen in the depiction of Las Vegas in *Diamonds Are Forever* (1971), an account based on filming there. The class location was important; the British casino that was shown was very much one at the apex of society, rather than the more mundane type of casino. The participants wore dinner jackets and used French terms for the game. Subsequently in *Dr. No*, Leiter provides an American presence in the very different world of the Caribbean.

Being a global brand entailed a range of considerations, including location, plot, action, characterization, and casting, notably using Gert Fröbe for Goldfinger, a choice that appealed to the German market even though he was the villain. These considerations all increasingly departed from British backgrounds in the 1960s, a key shift in the films from *From Russia, With Love* (1963) to *Diamonds Are Forever* (1971). This was a change, occurring across a few years, that registered the transformation and, in many respects, decline of Britain, and certainly of Britain as traditionally understood. In the former film, Bond realizes that the British agent he apparently met at Belgrade, an agent impersonated by "Red Grant," a villain played by Robert Shaw, is a fake because, for their meal on the train on the way toward the Italian frontier, he orders red wine with his fish. This is a flaw very much located in the traditional British class system, which still appeared valid in 1963, although it is painful now to listen to. In *Diamonds Are Forever*, Blofeld comments that irrelevant Britain is not even threatened. However, Bond saves the day and Washington. The global Bond brand can therefore survive the crisis of British power and still save the "big brother," who continues to need British ingenuity to survive.

To an unprecedented degree, the world of espionage powerfully grasped the twentieth-century imagination, not least as an alternative to large-scale industrial warfare. As with detective fiction, which can be seen not so much as a parallel literature but rather as the seedbed of the espionage novel, and notably of the British one, Britain played a central role in the new field. The key figure in the fictional world of British intelligence, a very crowded world, is Bond. His success has led not only to longevity, but also to a character that has spanned the worlds of novels and films. Fictional characters who have a long lifespan, such as Bond, who first appeared in 1953, provide an opportunity for the historian to study change; at the same time that the use of the character requires consistency, not least for the ready identification that will help the story to work, there is also a need to respond to the shifting expectations or concerns of the audience.

Bond himself did not emerge on a blank page—far from it. "Number One" among Agatha Christie's *Big Four* (1927) is an all-powerful Chinaman, Li Chang Yen, with his base in the mountain fastness of the Felsenlabyrinth in Switzerland, a country that was also significant to the plots of Holmes and Bond. Li Chang Yen echoes the sinister orientalism focused on, and strengthened by, Dr. Fu-Manchu, as well as his American-created counterparts. The brainchild of the British reporter Arthur Sarsfield, who wrote under the pseudonym Sax Rohmer, Fu-Manchu, "the greatest genius which the powers of evil have put on the earth for centuries," was the foe of British civilization and empire in a series of novels beginning with the absorbing *The Mystery of Dr Fu-Manchu* (1913) and *The Devil Doctor* (1916). He combined great cruelty with advanced scientific research. In an unambiguous geopolitical framing, Fu-Manchu, "the yellow peril incarnate in one man," is presented as a figure behind anti-Western actions in Hong Kong and Chinese Turkestan, as well as striking at Western politicians and administrators aware of the secret importance of Tongking, Mongolia, and Tibet; indeed, "he has found a new keyhole to the gate of the Indian Empire!" India was then crucial to Britain's international position. The omnipotence and range of the villain were such that, crucially in addition, no one in Britain was safe:

A veritable octopus had fastened upon England—a yellow octopus whose head was that of Dr Fu-Manchu, whose tentacles were dacoity, thuggee modes of death, secret and swift, which in the darkness plucked men from life and left no clue behind.

In his account of Macao in *Thrilling Cities* (1963), essentially an interesting episodic travelogue, Fleming wrote of his "Doctor Fu-Manchu days . . . the adventure books of one's youth," and in *Dr. No* (1958) he created, in Julius No, the villain, his very own Fu-Manchu. No's background is described at length in the novel, an element not captured in the film. Furthermore, with No, Bond, like Poirot in *The Big Four*, has to hunt the villain down in his base hidden within a mountain. *Fu-Manchu* was translated to the screen, new films continuing in the 1960s, as with *The Face of Fu Manchu* (1965).

Adventure books revealing Fleming's reading turn up in the Bond stories, both explicitly and implicitly. In *Moonraker* (1955), Gala Brand referred to "people that Phillips Oppenheim had dreamed up with fast cars and special cigarettes with gold bands on them and shoulder-holsters." This, in practice, is a description of Bond. Moreover, his Bentley was a reference to "Bulldog" Drummond's identical car in the Sapper stories. E. Phillips Oppenheim (1866–1946) was an English novelist who wrote a series of very successful adventure novels.

The hostile view of the Chinese seen in the Fu-Manchu stories was matched by a more general racism in early-twentieth-century adventure stories, British, American, and more generally. In the United States in 1935, John P. Marquand (1893–1960) published his first Mr. Moto story, with the Japanese detective of that name as the hero. In general, however, the writers of adventure and detective stories had clear prejudices. In Britain, in Freeman Wills Crofts's *The Pit-Prop Syndicate* (1922), the heroic Inspector Willis of Scotland Yard is described as meeting a restaurant manager, "a sly, evil-looking person seemingly of Semitic blood," later referred to as a German Jew. Once Willis leans on him, he is able to get the manager to be reasonable, but Willis is presented as having to bully him. This was typical of a language and approach that was no longer generally acceptable after 1945, but that affected Fleming's depiction of the villains, notably the Continental European ones, especially Auric Goldfinger and Ernst Stavro Blofeld, the head of SPECTRE. Like Drax, Goldfinger claims to be British, but Bond detects foreignness in the form of his being a "Balt," while his shortness and lack of proportion are also seen as symptomatic of trouble. This depiction of the villain is another aspect of the Fleming stories that today appears unacceptable.

Moreover, with another reference to a sinister "East," Goldfinger has an Oriental henchman in the shape of Oddjob. He is physically threatening, both in the novel and in the film, indeed a physical presence to match Goldfinger's menacing determination to plan a miracle of endeavor in crime. Furthermore, Oddjob looks indestructible. He is also threatening because he is out of place, and thus an aspect of the irruption of disorder that villainy feeds on, uses, and leads to. Oddjob is introduced as Goldfinger's chauffeur: "a chunky, flat-faced Japanese, or more probably Korean, with a wild, almost mad glare in dramatically slanting eyes that belonged in a Japanese film rather than in a Rolls-Royce on a sunny afternoon in Kent." This characterization is solidified when Oddjob is allowed a cat to strangle and eat; not the norm among chauffeurs. After World War II, in which many had served in the Japanese army, Koreans had a reputation for cruelty, notably due to the treatment of British prisoners of war.

Foreignness and the war were not only central factors for Fleming. His concern with Nazis and his sense of Britain as under threat were also seen with other writers, for example John Blackburn in his *A Scent of New-Mown Hay* (1958), a work paperbacked by Penguin in 1961. This brought together former SS members, the evil Fraulein Rosa Steinberg, a Himmler protégé who passes herself off as a Briton, and a conspiracy to destroy humanity by biological means, radiation and cell change. One of the heroes, General Kirk of "British Secret Intelligence" like Bond, drives a Bentley. The plot makes those of Fleming look credible.

The Bond stories repeatedly, in their plots and their details, chart changing images of Britain and the world, not least because the clear presentation of evil afoot served to record changing threats. The politics of *Casino Royale* were located squarely in the Cold War, with an attempt to thwart Soviet influence in the French trade unions. Indeed, in 1947, Major-General William "Wild Bill" Donovan (1883–1959), the former head of the Office of Strategic Services, whom Fleming had dealt with during the war, had helped persuade the American government to fund opposition to Communist influence in these unions.

In the novel, Bond's attempt to out-gamble his Communist opponent, Le Chiffre, is rescued by Felix Leiter, the CIA observer, who loans him thirty-two million (old) francs, with which Bond subsequently beats the villain. Le Chiffre is the paymaster of the Communist-controlled trade union in the heavy and transport industries of Alsace, which was the most vulnerable part of France to Soviet attack, and one that is crucial to the NATO response to any such attack. Without permission, Le Chiffre had invested fifty million francs of trade union funds in a network of French brothels, only for a new law against brothels to wreck his investment.

There was considerable sensitivity in Britain at the time about the extent of Communist influence in the trade unions. In 1949, the Labour government had sent in troops to deal with a London dock strike that it blamed on Communists. The following year, Hugh Gaitskell, the Minister of Fuel and Power, claimed that a strike in the power stations was instigated by Communist shop stewards and served for them as a rehearsal for future confrontation. Gaitskell became leader of the Labour Party in 1955, serving as such until his premature death in 1963. As Fleming was aware, Gaitskell, by then, was the lover of his wife, Ann.

Bond's need for the American money in *Casino Royale* reflected the central role of the United States in the defense of the West, which was readily apparent due to the events of World War II and the strength of the Red Army. Leiter provides the money without difficulty and is happy to rely on Bond's skill, suggesting a far simpler and smoother working of the alliance than was in fact the case. The two powers were cooperating in NATO and the UK-US Security Agreement covering signals espionage, and had fought together in Korea. As part of the deterrence against Soviet attack, American nuclear bombers were based in Britain.

However, there were serious differences of opinion, particularly over the Middle East, where America had followed a very different policy to Britain over Palestine/Israel. More generally, the American government repeatedly made clear its view that the European empires, including that of Britain, were anachronistic and that the United States should align with anti-colonial movements in order to keep them away from Communism. Furthermore, American concern over the British spy system had risen greatly after the defections to the Soviet Union of Guy Burgess and Donald Maclean in 1951. In addition, in 1952, well-founded distrust of Kim Philby, the Secret Services liaison officer in Washington, led the CIA to insist that he not return there. This concern continued.

Fleming did not press Anglo-American tensions in his novels, notably over espionage, but he was well aware of them. Indeed, they were to the fore in *You Only Live Twice* (1964), where America's sidelining of Britain in the Pacific world was important to the story. At times, Fleming's plots can be seen as a response, or, at least, as efforts to create an impression of the normality of British imperial rule and action, with Bond as the defender of empire. The plots also reflected the attempted management of the world into a form of Anglo-American condominium in which British skill helped American power. In response to the rift during the Suez Crisis of 1956, this was a key theme of the foreign policy of Harold Macmillan, prime minister from 1957 to 1963, and, like Fleming, an Old Etonian.

In the second novel, *Live and Let Die* (1954), Fleming presented the United States as threatened. Responding to strong interest among British readers in the United States and to the market there for his books, and potentially for films, Fleming did not become formulaic by repeating the setting of his first novel. This, indeed, was to be one of his strong features, contrasting with the repeated settings used by most other writers of the genre, from Eric Ambler to John Le Carré. In *Casino Royale*, the use of the fictional Royale, a luxurious European gambling resort, which was modeled on Deauville and Le Touquet in France and on Estoril in Portugal, was a throwback to the locations of interwar novels. This was not least with the villain being a deracinated European: Le Chiffre is described as part Jewish, with some Mediterranean, Prussian, or Polish blood added into the mix.

Instead, in *Live and Let Die*, Fleming now offered the New World, with Britain, in the person of Bond, active in it, and presented his agent as moving there by aircraft, not the ocean liners used so frequently in prewar novels. In place of the tired, cloying opulence of the casino at Royale at 3:00 a.m., *Live and Let Die* opened with the movement, energy, and luxury of a welcomed arrival at Idlewild (now JFK) airport in New York. This was a scene based on Fleming's arrivals there in 1941 and 1953, and one that would have been unfamiliar to the vast majority of British readers. Scheduled passenger air services across the Atlantic had only begun in 1939, before being interrupted by the war and only resuming thereafter.

Thanks to aircraft, Bond is able to travel at will and at speed across the globe, and the novels were very much part of the air age, as were the plots; although the glamor of long-distance train journeys also played a role, including in *Live and Let Die* where the rail journey from New York to Miami is described in an impressive piece of writing. *From Russia, With Love* also uses a famous rail route, that of the Orient Express. In later novels, Bond flies to Tokyo and to the West Indies, and in the films he generally arrives by aircraft. In the first film, *Dr. No*, Bond flies to Kingston, Jamaica, via New York, his arrival and collection at the airport being both shown and significant in the plot.

Driving in from Idlewild in *Live and Let Die*, Bond remarks that New York "must be the fattest atomic-bomb target on the whole face of the world," and Black Power is presented as the tool of Soviet subversion. Its leader, the sinister Mr. Big, "the head of the Black Widow Voodoo cult" and a member of the Soviet espionage network SMERSH, has Bond seized subsequently in Harlem. America is highly vulnerable. In response to the suggestion that Mr. Big be arrested, the FBI warns that this would lead to a race riot. Bond "felt his spine crawl at the cold, brilliant efficiency of the Soviet machine." Later in the novel, he reflects:

> Never before in his life had there been so much to play for. The secret of the treasure, the defeat of a great criminal, the smashing of a Communist spy ring, and the destruction of a tentacle of SMERSH, the cruel machine that was his own private target. And now Solitaire, the ultimate personal prize.

And, immediately following, a wonderfully enigmatic phrase: "The stars winked down their cryptic morse and he had no keys to their cipher." Fleming could certainly coin images and phrases.

Live and Let Die concluded in the Caribbean, providing Bond with his first visit (in the novels) to the British Empire and helping establish the Bond world as a travelogue. In this Fleming competed with his elder brother Peter, a noted travel writer. Part of the popularity of the Bond books related to the idea of being able to travel at will and at speed across the globe. An important aspect of the politics and geopolitics of the novels, and one that did not translate to the films, was that Fleming's Bond was in part a defender of empire. This is a strand that tends to be lost with reference to Bond as a figure of the Cold War, and his location in terms of the struggle with the Soviets. That dimension was of course significant, but it is necessary also to consider what was being defended. For Fleming and his British readers, this was the British Empire. To them, opposition to the Soviet Union was not separate to the defense of empire. In his own copy of the novel, Fleming recorded, "All the settings are based on personal experience and I spent a whole night in Harlem with a detective from the 10th precinct verifying my geography etc. The underwater chapters are based on Cabritta Island etc."

In the fourth novel, *Diamonds Are Forever* (1956), Bond returns to the United States, appealing to British interest in a land of wealth and excitement, as well as America's role as a model for consumer society. Commercial television had started in Britain in 1955, and that helped to make advertisements and the American settings of soap operas very present to the British public. Again, however, there is an enemy within. Fighting the Mafia in *Diamonds Are Forever* provided Fleming with an opportunity to express the racist views of the interwar years: "They're not Americans. Mostly a lot of Italian bums with monogrammed shirts who spend the day eating spaghetti and meat-balls and squirting scent over themselves," a clear sign of contemporary British views on masculinity. However, Jack and Seraffimo Spang, the gangsters of the film, are not convincing villains, nor is their villainy particularly interesting or threatening. This is a far less impressive novel than *Live and Let Die*. In his copy of *Diamonds*, Fleming noted that he had lost $500 in Las Vegas.

Here, as with the Cold War, it is important to move from an abstraction to the specifics of particular moments. The Cold War, for example, meant very different situations throughout the 1950s, let alone over a longer time span of Bond's appearances. For example, in 1952, when Fleming was writing *Casino Royale*, Britain was providing the second-biggest contingent in the UN force that had intervened in the Korean War, while the continuation of the conscription introduced for World War II meant that the book was being written for readers many of whom had served in the war or were still serving—points also true of friends and relatives.

The situation was different by the end of the 1950s. Then conscription was on the way out and the burden of defense against Communism was largely placed on missiles. Indeed, that defensive capacity was to underline the rocketry that played a major role in three of the first six Bond films (with atomic bombs being central to the plot of another). The Soviet launch of *Sputnik* in 1957 appeared to make the entire world vulnerable to atomic warheads delivered by intercontinental ballistic rockets and certainly made the public aware of this point. In practice, the development and deployment of these weapons and delivery systems took several years, and atomic bombs dropped from aircraft remained crucial, but Fleming frequently dealt with developing technology, as well as what was to come or likely to come. This was a characteristic shared by the films. At any rate, the Cuban missile crisis of 1962 between the United States and the Soviet Union helped make the threat of nuclear war a very real one.

Similarly, empire meant different situations in particular years. From the perspective of the 2010s, there is a misleading theme of gradual and inevitable descent from imperial status, and the emphasis is on Britain's willingness to concede independence and on the generally peaceful nature of the process. Indeed, in 1947, Britain had granted independence to India, its most populous colony, which became the countries of India and Pakistan, and in 1948, Burma (Myanmar), Ceylon (Sri Lanka), Palestine (Israel), and Newfoundland rapidly followed. However, although India had, of all the "non-white" colonies, most engaged the imaginative attention of the British, its loss was not seen as part of an inevitable process of rapid imperial withdrawal. On the contrary, there were attempts to strengthen both formal and informal empire in the late 1940s and early 1950s, while it was believed that most colonies were far from ready for independence. Particular effort was devoted to protecting the imperial position in Malaya, where Britain successfully overcame a Chinese-backed Communist insurrection, in a struggle that involved conflict in the years of the early Bond novels. Britain also sought to strengthen the economy of the British colonies in Africa, and also very much remained the imperial presence in the Persian Gulf, deploying troops to protect Kuwait against Iraqi invasion in 1961. Three years earlier, troops had been sent to Jordan. It was believed in Britain that the African and Pacific colonies would not be ready for independence for many decades, a belief that reflected racist views.

Bond's main beat, however, was not that of imperial policeman, thwarting insurrection in Malaya, Kenya, or Cyprus, or protecting British interests against nationalists, notably in Iran, as in 1951, and, later, Egypt, especially in 1956 during the Suez Crisis. Instead, Fleming located empire in the wider context of British strategic interests and did so, significantly, with reference to the West's position in the Cold War. This was clearly seen in *Live and Let Die* when, in pursuit of Mr. Big, Bond travels to Jamaica, which Fleming had first visited in World War II, and is briefed by Commander John Strangways, the chief Secret Service agent for the West Indies, a character assassinated in *Dr. No*. This briefing is about the Isle of Surprise, an offshore island recently purchased by Mr. Big. Readers were offered a defined and informed sense of strategic threat:

> Since 1950 Jamaica had become an important strategic target, thanks to the development by Reynolds Metal and the Kaiser Corporation of huge bauxite deposits found on the island. So far as Strangways was concerned, the activities on Surprise might easily be the erection of a base for one-man submarines in the event of war, particularly since Shark Bay was within range of the route followed by the Reynolds ships to the new bauxite harbour at Ocho Rios, a few miles down the coast.

Bauxite was necessary for the manufacture of aluminum, a strategic metal, not least for the aircraft industry and for missile production; the companies mentioned were American ones. At this stage of the Cold War, the delivery of nuclear weaponry was very much from aircraft, and this capability was regarded as crucial to the American ability to counter Soviet superiority on land and, thereby, to protect Western Europe, which was the theme of *Casino Royale*. Fleming was writing in the strategic shadow of World War II, with its revelation, in 1940, that Britain was highly vulnerable if a hostile power dominated Continental Europe to a degree far greater than before the age of mass airpower. In 1940, it was Germany, but by the time of Fleming's novels, it was the Soviet Union, although Germany, or, at least Germans, remained a threat as far as Fleming was concerned.

In *Live and Let Die*, Bond is revealed as already knowing Jamaica; he had spent time there assigned to protect local labor unions from Communist infiltration. This was a typical sign of the seamless transition for Fleming from fighting Nazis to combating Communism—one in which his generation was located. Fleming was not troubled with detail: as part of the empire, Jamaica for intelligence purposes came under E Branch of MI5, so the fictional Bond would have had to be seconded to it. The reference to Mr. Big's plans links the defense of the British empire to that of American interests, both in the Caribbean and in North America.

The Conservative Prime Minister in 1955–1957, Anthony Eden, another Old Etonian, was part of Fleming's social circle. Bond returned to the empire at the close of *Diamonds Are Forever* (1956), killing the last of the villains in Sierra Leone, whose "great diamond mines" were "a rich capital asset of the British Commonwealth," and then again in *Dr. No* (1958), where Crab Key, another island off Jamaica, holds a dark secret. At the close of the latter, there is a display of British imperial power. The brigadier in command of the Caribbean Defence Force, "a modern young soldier of thirty-five . . . unimpressed by relics from the Edwardian era of Colonial Governors, whom he collectively referred to as 'feather-hatted fuddy-duddies,'" pressed for immediate action without waiting for London. He was ready to provide a platoon that would be embarked on HMS *Narvik*, a warship whose name recalled a major World War II British naval success against the Germans in Norwegian waters, and in 1940, before the United States came into the war. The youthfulness and vigor of the brigadier, who would have been too young to serve in that war, suggested that the empire was not moribund and that it still had a capable military that could act worldwide. Bond was not alone. Instead, he was a key element in a broader defense profile.

However, in *Dr. No*, there was also a strong sense of threat, as when the bastion of colonial rule in the capital, Kingston, is discussed: "Such stubborn retreats will not long survive in modern Jamaica. One day Queen's Club will have its windows smashed and perhaps be burned to the ground." This threat is not that of Dr. No, SMERSH, or SPECTRE; but, rather, that of the nationalism already destabilizing British colonies, most notably the Gold Coast (Ghana), which gained independence in 1957, but also elsewhere, for example, in the Caribbean region, both in Grenada and nearby, in British Guiana. Indeed, troops were deployed in both cases. Sierra Leone itself gained independence in 1961, and Jamaica in 1962.

In *Dr. No*, Bond thwarts a Soviet-backed attempt to bring down American rockets. A sense of America under threat is also clear in the novel *Goldfinger* (1959): the Superintendent at Pennsylvania Station in New York tells Goldfinger that travelers from Louisville report being sprayed from the air by the Soviets. If, in this novel, Bond saves the American gold reserves, which are held at Fort Knox, the old world coming to the aid of the stronger new, he is also all that Britain can rely on after failure in the Suez Crisis of 1956. By *Goldfinger*, Bond was a representative of a shift from brawn to brains, resources to skill, with the latter seen by the British government as crucial to the management of relations with the United States. In October 1957, after the Bermuda and Washington Anglo-American conferences, Harold Macmillan, the British prime minister, claimed to have regained the special relationship with the United States after the fundamental division during the Suez Crisis when American pressure had played a major role in the British climbdown. Macmillan was an exponent of the emphasis on skill, referring to Britain as taking a position like Classical Greece to the Rome of the modern United States. On November 14, 1957, Macmillan informed the British Cabinet that the "Declaration of Common Purpose" he had signed with Eisenhower in Washington on October 25 was

> a declaration of interdependence, recognising that the old concept of national self-sufficiency is out of date and that the countries of the Free World can maintain their security only by combining their resources and sharing their tasks. The United Kingdom and the United States Governments have agreed to act henceforward in accordance with this principle.

This was to be the world of the Bond films and notably of Connery's and of the first Moore one. However, in practice, the British position as outlined by Macmillan was precarious, as well as arrogant, not least because of the weakness of the British economy, a weakness that the Americans rightly considered a major issue. Fleming understood this precariousness.

Competition and tension with the United States also echoed in the Bond stories, although this theme was not pushed. In the short story "Quantum of Solace," published as part of *Five Secret Occasions in the Life of James Bond* (1960), for example, there is mention of Anglo-American competition on the Nassau–New York air route. Those of Fleming's generation were well aware of such tensions and in Fleming's case there was a cultural element. This was seen in his critical description of New York hotels in his piece "007 in New York," published in the *New York Herald Tribune* in October 1963: "those sighing lifts, the rooms full of last month's air and a vague memory of ancient cigars, the empty 'You're welcomes,' the thin coffee . . . the dank toast." In practice, many British hotels had a range of problems, while there was no level below which British cooking could not fall.

The British need to adapt to America was an important, albeit concealed, theme in the politics of the novels and films. For the British, at the same time, it was important that America see them as allies who would be supported in Western Europe and the Empire. Britain wished to be treated by the United States as a dependable, but independent, ally. This was a difficult position and one that was far easier for Bond to negotiate than for British governments. The need to adapt was more generally true of British culture, and it is to the culture of this period that we turn in the next chapter.

2

CHANGING VALUES

James Bond, with two double bourbons inside him, sat in the final departure lounge of Miami Airport and thought about life and death.

The one-sentence, one-paragraph, start to *Goldfinger* (1959) is very different from the world of the films. However, it captures the essence of the novels. Alongside adventure stories, these are accounts of life and death. Moreover, they offer Fleming an approach that is denied the filmmakers, that in addition gives greater depth to his story and creation: he can present ideas and observations as if from himself, and also from Bond.

Depth, of course, is a comparative term with Bond, and, indeed, with any adventure hero, but there is certainly more depth than is suggested by the films. Indeed, the contrast between the start of the novels and the abrupt adventure beginnings of the films is very clear. In many respects, the films act on the basis that Bond is both well known and a fixed personality, while the novels assume that his personality has to be sketched out and that the character develops. Thus, at the beginning of *Goldfinger*, Bond reflects on his professional status as a killer and on the nature of death, in the person of his killing of a Mexican assassin. Regret, however, is rejected as the "death-watch beetle in the soul," a judgment that can be seen as pure Fleming.

This passage leads Bond to consider the equivalent of the pre-film action sequence. This consideration is a fairly well informed and coherent discussion of how international crime was conducted. Fleming presents the world of opium taking in Mexico as affected by a British ban on heroin, which encourages an increase of drug smuggling into Britain. Bond is instructed to destroy the channel at its source. He flattens the drug warehouse, watching from a café as the bomb blows it up, in a scene echoed in the film. A drug-addled Mexican then tries to knife him, but Bond kills him with two blows described in detail, one the standby of the wartime commandos. During the war, Fleming had directed 30 Assault Unit, a commando group sent on intelligence missions. The comparable episode in the film has a sex interest as well as relaxing humor at its close about the "shocking" electrocution of this villain. Killing and death are more realistic in the novels.

The killing leaves Bond wanting the relief of drunkenness in a fashion not seen in the films, as well as describing his sex life in a particularly harsh light: "get drunk, stinking drunk so that he would have to be carried to bed by whatever tart he had picked up." This is presented as a necessary relief from a world of kill or be killed. This world leads to a series of reflections offered as a morbid reaction to a "dirty assignment." Fleming is advancing a psychological realism akin to that which Agatha Christie provided in her detective novels. This was not a realism that Fleming's critics liked—nor the filmmakers. In the films, the women were stunning, the filmmakers creating an image that the grittier novels do not necessarily match.

The mood in the novel then abruptly shifts to the meeting at the airport with Junius Du Pont, a middle-aged American whose clothes are reported in great detail. Only Fleming could feel it appropriate to locate men in this fashion: "The rolled ends of the collar were joined by a gold safety pin beneath the knots of a narrow dark red and blue striped tie that fractionally wasn't the Brigade of Guards," the elite unit in the British army. That is not an approach that would be seen today, nor would Bond's dislike of proffered lighters. Instead, Bond emerges as a snob. And then Bond is off to help Du Pont at his Miami hotel where he has to deal with a card cheat. This turns out to be the introduction to Goldfinger, a man, on the pattern of Drax in *Moonraker*, whose sinister scheme is ruined by a fatal flaw in his character.

The Bond world reflects our changing values and those of the last sixty-five years. It is a mirror, indeed, on our world, and a mirror that many of us look into. This is true of the details of Bond's life and also of the values he represents. Both are central to his thrilling adventures. The changing representation of goodness, value, and virtue, specifically the tension between traditional and more self-consciously modern moral concerns, is particularly relevant in our response to heroes. This is because Bond, the fictional hero of our age, is portrayed as a servant of good in what are generally deeply moral, even Manichean, texts: evil exists and needs to be not just resisted but defeated.

The Bond corpus stretches across the great breach of the 1960s, and had to respond to it. This breach destroyed a cultural continuity in Britain, the United States, and elsewhere, that had lasted from the Victorian period. This destruction reflected the impact of social and ideological trends, including the rise of new cultural forms and a new agenda molded by self-conscious shifts in the understanding of gender, sexuality, youth, class, place, and race, for example, of the sexual revolution of the 1960s.

This breach indeed was a challenge to the presentation of Bond because, as originally portrayed, he was very much a figure of the early 1950s, written by a man whose ideas were prewar, and one produced for a readership that was in the shadow of world war, indeed of two world wars. In Bond, Fleming created a

rock-hard war-hero type, an image of toughness, sharpness, reso-
luteness, cleverness, and male sexuality that he wanted to identify
anew with the British after the disruption of World War II and
the Labour governments of 1945–1951, to which he was hostile.
Bond's character and virtues were displayed in his actions: he
represented, and defined, a notion of gentlemanliness understood
as action, and not as a set of empty conventions. Thus, his gentlemanly virtues were seen to include sportsmanship and being an
all-rounder, virtues not associated with the Labour Party nor with
the norms linked to the Festival of Britain it had sponsored in
1951. Labour, indeed, was far more urban and working-class in its
focus than Fleming's gentlemanly values.

With his combination of gentlemanly virtues and decisiveness,
Bond represented the values and self-image of manly courage of
the officer class in the British armed forces, a class much on show
in the British films of the 1950s, as in David Lean's classic *Bridge
on the River Kwai* (1957). Indeed, the war is frequently referred
to, both directly and indirectly, in the Fleming novels. Thus, on
the way to M's offices in *Thunderball* there came "a continuous
machine-gun rattle and clack from the cipher machines." Miss
Moneypenny "liked what she called the shot-and-shell days." One
of the villains, Giuseppe Petacchi in *Thunderball*, an Italian air-
man entrusted with German pressure mines during the war, had
killed the pilot and the navigator before handing over his aircraft
and its mines to the Allies, and been rewarded accordingly. Dr.
No is described as running Crab Key "like a concentration camp."
In turn, Bond was like a stylish commando, able to set his own
rules, but guaranteed to do so in a fair fashion, and to worthwhile
ends.

There is change alongside continuity, but they can be recon-
ciled. "M had never approved of Bond's womanising. It was
anathema to his Victorian soul" (*Goldfinger*). Yet, presenting what
Fleming sees as a benign system of authority, the two men under-

stand each other. Fleming, however, was fairly clear in his views on the Victorians. He backed a degree of change. For example, in "Quantum of Solace," a gripping short story published in 1960, the governor of the Bahamas comments on a colleague in the British Colonial Service:

> His emotional life ran along the frustrated and unhealthy lines that were part of our inheritance from our Victorian grandfathers . . . he was sadly ignorant of sexual matters. Not a rare thing even today among young people in England, but very common in those days, and the cause . . . of many—very many—disastrous marriages and other tragedies. . . . Perhaps Masters's father and mother were the true guilty people. They turned Masters into an accident-prone man.

Britain and its empire in 1953 was a world relatively secure in purpose but, nevertheless, greatly under challenge. From the outset, Bond, a hero in its defense, is not shown fighting decent people, but, instead, people who are trying to blow up a gale to bring down the world, to employ a phrase Fleming quoted. Bond might like to present himself as a stylish cog, but although both are very important, he is given purpose neither by his profession nor by the secret service, but by the morality and righteousness of the wider struggle in which he figures. This is a point very much brought out at the end of the first novel, *Casino Royale* (1953). Evil was afoot, and while the sense of evil was not that of one of Denis Wheatley's black-magic novels, notably *The Devil Rides Out* (1934), this sense was more atmospheric in *Casino Royale* than in the subsequent Bond stories, other than the pervasive voodoo of the film *Live and Let Die* (1973). *The Devil Rides Out* was filmed in 1968 with Charles Gray and Christopher Lee, both actors who starred as Bond villains: in *Diamonds Are Forever* and *Man with the Golden Gun*, respectively.

The inherent seriousness of the early-1950s Bond novels, a seriousness very much at odds with the semicomic irony of the

Roger Moore presentation of Bond on screen from 1973 to 1985, Moore as the comic anti-Bond, was a reflection of much of contemporary British culture. The bleak political satires of another Old Etonian (albeit before Fleming), George Orwell, in *Animal Farm* (1945) and *Nineteen Eighty-Four* (1949), had made a considerable impact. Carol Reed's film *The Third Man* (1949) was set not in the future, but in a corrupt and devastated present where occupied Vienna could serve to suggest similarities to austerity-era Britain. The screenplay was by Graham Greene, who, in his novel *The Heart of the Matter* (1948), had also tackled the failure to maintain moral standards in the face of a pitiless world. Although the two men fell out in 1960, Fleming greatly admired Greene's work, notably in spy fiction. *Brideshead Revisited* (1945), a novel by Evelyn Waugh, a friend and correspondent of Fleming's wife, also dealt with faith assailed and the dangers of hedonism and democratization. *The Third Man* was echoed in many later films, including the Bond film *The Living Daylights* (1987), which was set in a modern Vienna.

Meanwhile, contemporary British music reflected a sense of tension, as the earlier music of Edward Elgar and Ralph Vaughan Williams was criticized as too nice or overly florid by influential young composers of the period, especially Benjamin Britten and Michael Tippett. Britten's operas, notably *Peter Grimes* (1945), *Billy Budd* (1951), and *The Turn of the Screw* (1954), were disturbing works. In contrast, the Ealing film comedies of the late 1940s and early 1950s, such as *Passport to Pimlico* (1949), *Kind Hearts and Coronets* (1949), and *The Lavender Hill Mob* (1951), were far less bleak, although their satire could not conceal the same sense that the world was rarely benign. The London of these comedies lacked the sleekness of the opulence and material comfort revealed in the London of the Bond novels. In practice, with its many bombsites and with the pervasive smoke, smell, and grime from its coal fires, London was grim.

On radio, Britain was challenged by sinister schemes that had to be thwarted by *Dick Barton, Special Agent* (1946–1951); he also starred in three British films of the period (1948–1950). Barton had a radio signature tune that was as atmospheric and gripping for his audience as the theme music of the Bond films was to be. The Boulting Brothers made the film *High Treason* (1951), about Communists trying to sabotage power stations, the nearest British equivalent to the Hollywood "Red Scare" films. This was the background to Bond, although Dick Barton scarcely had the sex interest or activity of Bond, nor the global appeal.

If the political context of Bond was clear, and the subsuming, by duty and need, of his troubled angst about the desirability of killing struck ready moral echoes for many readers, Bond's social position was also assured in the 1950s. He was affluent and his stylishness betokened class, and class in a world that understood social distinctions. Bond's ready popularity also reflected the widespread popularity of narrative. Public libraries continued to buy and lend large quantities of Agatha Christie and other secure genre writers. The successful staples of the West End stage in this period also reflected continuity. Audiences flocked to see plays by Fleming's friend Noel Coward, both old (such as *Private Lives*, 1930) and new (for example, *Look After Lulu*, 1959), as well as new plays by the wartime playwright Terence Rattigan (*The Winslow Boy*, 1946) and by William Douglas-Home (*The Chiltern Hundreds*, 1947; *The Manor of Northstead*, 1954). The audiences were also very large for the short stories Agatha Christie adapted for the stage: *The Mousetrap* (1952) and *Witness for the Prosecution* (1953).

Yet, by the late 1950s, there was a far stronger challenge in Britain to the conventional mores and values seen with Fleming. The novelists of the 1940s had been concerned, at times despairing, but not generally angry. The late 1950s, in contrast, were to be the stage for the "Angry Young Men," a group of writers who felt very much at odds with their Britain. Their problems were not those of faith in a hostile world (the issues addressed by Greene and Waugh), nor the pressure for totalitarianism that worried Orwell. Instead, they reflected a disaffection with society. Specifically, the "Angry Young Men" had a sense that the postwar reforms of the Labour governments and, subsequently, the 1950s affluence, linked to the Conservative governments and indeed to Bond, had produced a vulgar, materialist society that was disagreeable in itself and frustrating to them as individuals. These writers were impatient alike with traditionalism and with the values of the new ITV, the commercial television with its advertisements, launched in 1955.

In contrast to Bond, or to the very different liberal worthiness of C. P. Snow's Lewis Eliot, the protagonist of his sequence of novels *Strangers and Brothers* (1940–1970), came Charles Lumley in John Wain's novel *Hurry on Down* (1953), a graduate who flees self-advancement and becomes a window cleaner, and Jim Dixon, the hapless protagonist in Kingsley Amis's *Lucky Jim* (1954). The latter novel also struck at the "phoniness" of social mores in the period. Social values were lacerated in John Osborne's aggressive and bitter play *Look Back in Anger* (1956), John Braine's novel *Room at the Top* (1957), Alan Sillitoe's novel *Saturday Night and Sunday Morning* (1958), and David Storey's novel *This Sporting Life* (1960).

Sillitoe's account of working-class life in his native Nottingham was an example of the "grim up north" [of England] school that became fashionable in the 1950s, a branch of realism that was self-consciously antithetical to the dominant social mores and to much of the cultural mainstream. This approach very much contrasted with Fleming's style. In 1962, he noted that the Bond novels had "no message for suffering humanity," but had been "written for warm-blooded heterosexuals in railways, trains, aeroplanes or beds." Nor was Fleming, who was critical of the "Angry

Young Men," interested in the north of England. Moreover, the Scotland Fleming echoed was that of John Buchan's engagement with the virtues of robust outdoor life, not the working-class industrial Scotland. Ironically, Fleming's *The Spy Who Loved Me* (1962) offered much social and psychological reality, although not set in the north of England. There was no incompatibility here between being serious and entertainment.

A stronger interest in the north of England had a number of manifestations in the early 1960s. Northern accents became fashionable, while northerners, such as the dramatist Alan Bennett and the Beatles, "made it" on the national scale, as, in 1964, did the Labour Party under another northerner, Harold Wilson, when it won the general election. In turn, heroism was repositioned and presented anew as the social and geographical location of style changed. The films of Marlon Brando had revealed the limitations of the British southern matinee idol. Now northern men (and Welsh men, such as Richard Burton) addressed this lack. When Bond went onto the screen in 1962 he was played, not, as Fleming had wanted, by the smooth, gentlemanly David Niven, but by a rough Scotsman, Sean Connery. Although produced by North Americans, this characterization was an aspect of the stronger interest in the north, here understood as including Scotland. Apart from everything else, Eon, the Bond filmmakers, had to reach out to the large audience in the north, although a film with Niven, a well-known actor, might have been more bankable than one with the "nobody" Connery.

At the start of the 1960s, morality in Britain (as in the United States and elsewhere) still had a strong collectivist dimension, with moral precepts enshrined in law and protected by policing. The disruptive consequences of individualism were abhorrent in a system that emphasized collective effort and provision, notably of healthcare. This was a result of the major impetus given to corporatism and socialism by the social mobilization deemed necessary to wage World War II, and to give effect to the policies of the postwar Labour governments. Not filling in forms, or not having a fixed address, was a defiance of a particularly powerful bureaucracy. In addition, the combination of prewar moral strictures and 1940s regimentation ensured that moral policing criminalized habits judged unacceptable, such as taking drugs. Abortion, homosexuality, prostitution, and suicide were criminal offenses. Restrictive divorce laws affected marriage, childcare, and sexuality. Censorship determined what could be read, seen, and listened to. Leisure activities, whether drinking, gambling, or watching television, were highly regulated.

This was the world of Fleming and his audience, not, in all respects, the world that they had inherited, but a world that brought together Victorian values with the impact of the tumultuous 1940s, first world war and then government controls and Socialist change. Alongside the disruption of the war and the Labour years, there was a widespread emphasis on continuity, and innovations and change were viewed warily. There was a nostalgia for the "good old days" alongside the quest for the bright lights. The Bond novels reflected some of this nostalgia. In *Goldfinger*, there is disdain for the villain's provision of "some curried mess [in fact shrimp] with rice." Indeed, Fleming and Bond were both conservative in their eating habits. Although discussed in the novels, food plays only a scant role in the films. Meals are of little consequence in them, barring the dinner on the train in *From Russia, With Love*. In the novels, the drinking and smoking were heavy but also socially acceptable for the day. The drinking and smoking of Bond as described in *Thunderball* in particular were heavy.

Writing in the shadow of World War II and for that generation, Fleming produced a romance that resonated. In some respects, Fleming and Bond were aspects of the Conservative reaction against Labour rule. The reaction was particularly seen in the end of rationing and in the embrace of affluence, notably with a

loosening of credit restrictions and the encouragement of borrow-
ing through hire purchase. The emphasis on material goods in the
Bond novels, the opulence in the life of a secret agent, matched
this moment, mood, and interest.

Yes, there was also a more profound sense that Fleming represented an older established code and set of values, both in his
fantasy and in his observations of British society, a new version of
that of the interwar years, with Bond, the last of the clubland
heroes, in a world in which their values still counted. This situation, however, was under pressure in the 1950s. Indeed, the novels were not only a throwback but also an aspect of the way in
which the 1950s prefigured much generally associated with the
1960s. Images of sex played a much greater role in life in the
1950s, not least in newspapers, novels, and films, than they had
done a decade earlier, or, at least, these images were more overt,
but changed fundamentally only in the 1960s, with a stress on the
individual, and on his or her ability to construct their own particular world. In Britain, the outcome of the *Lady Chatterley* trial,
with Penguin Books acquitted in 1962 of the charge of obscenity
for publishing D. H. Lawrence's novel, signaled that the new
decade would be one of change.

Change indeed rapidly followed, gathering pace from 1963 on-
ward, a year of sexual liberation, as Philip Larkin noted. This was
a period in which fashions, such as the miniskirt and popular
music, both stressed novelty. Songs and films, such as *Tom Jones*
(1963) and *Darling* (1965), featured sexual independence. This
aspect of the period affected the presentation of the Bond corpus,
particularly when the novels were translated to the screen, and
notably in their depiction of sexual relationships. To a degree,
although starting in 1973, the Moore films captured the tone of
these years, including an ironical, if not satirical, strand. In
contrast, Connery's more traditional style reflected the beginning
of the 1960s. Indeed, in the film *Goldfinger*, Bond criticizes

drinking champagne below a certain temperature, saying it is "as bad as listening to the Beatles without earmuffs."

The hedonism of the 1960s, or rather the mid- to late 1960s, focused on free will, self-fulfillment, and consumerism, and the last was the motor of economic consumption and growth. The net effect was a more multifaceted public construction of individual identities. This stress on individual identities did not lend itself to a classification of identity, interest, and activity in terms of traditional social categories, especially class distinctions.

Instead, there was an emphasis on style as the means, and even goal, of social definition. For young males, this emphasis powerfully contributed to the appeal of the Bond corpus, although there was no Bond style in clothing as opposed to the significant branding of particular items. Both novels and films were replete with style themes, notably in dress and cars, and, more generally, in how the hero moves, smokes, and talks to women.

The Bond corpus also captures attention as an instance of another controverted virtue, that of cultural quality as defined by public bodies. These tended, in the 1950s, to view mass culture with dismay, a position particularly taken on the Left. Socialists had long sought not only equality of opportunity and the more equal distribution of wealth, but also to transform the working class into a moral, united, and educated force. They hoped for self-improvement and "rational" recreation, not the bright lights and/or rowdiness and vulgarity of football or music hall that the working class was looking toward. In the Bond novels, the emphasis is on enjoyment, and enjoyment for the moment. In contrast, self-improvement through attacking enjoyment is criticized by being advocated by Goldfinger, a killjoy whose views, ironically, have become the orthodoxy in the West. He did not smoke or drink, characterizing smoking as "entirely against nature. Can you imagine a cow or any animal taking a mouthful of smoldering straw then breathing in the smoke and blowing it out through its nostrils? Pah!" The name Goldfinger is significant; Fleming based it on Erno Goldfinger, an aggressively Modernist architect of Continental extraction.

In Britain, the question of how to view, and even direct, mass culture played a key role in the debate over state intervention in culture. This intervention was an aspect of a culture war between the criteria and ranking set by the artistic Establishment that very much influenced and directed government funding, and, in contrast, criteria and ranking that made sense of, and responded to, the culture of popular taste. The latter was the culture in which Bond was located and very deliberately so. This culture war led, and still leads, to issues of taste and influence that divided commentators. Were, for example, the most influential and "best" novels of the 1950s the Bond novels, or the early novels of Iris Murdoch, for example *Under the Net* (1954) and *The Bell* (1958)?

Whatever judgments are made, it is the case that the latter type of work tended, and tends, to attract far more attention from critics and intellectuals. That, indeed, was central to the cultural politics of the century. British critics, such as Q. D. Leavis in *Fiction and the Reading Public*, were skeptical of, if not hostile to, bestsellers, and Fleming was a clear and obvious target. He became more popular as his books were serialized as a strip cartoon in the *Daily Express* from 1957 to 1962, then Britain's leading circulation newspaper. This began with *From Russia, With Love*. However, the Bond corpus faced bitter attacks in Britain, the most famous and frequently cited being Paul Johnson's piece "Sex, Snobbery and Sadism," published on April 5, 1958, in the *New Statesman*, then a respectable, left-wing British literary journal with wide appeal. Condemning *Dr. No* (1958) as "the nastiest book" he had read, which said a lot about his limited reading and his flawed judgment, Johnson described its essential contents as: "all unhealthy, all thoroughly English: the sadism of a schoolboy bully, the mechanical two-dimensional sex-longings of a frustrated adolescent, and the crude, snob-cravings of a suburban adult." "Thoroughly English" was then a term Johnson would have employed as an insult, which tells you a lot about the attitudes of left-wing writers at the time, and, indeed, today as cosmopolitanism is their major theme. Johnson himself has become a pillar of the Right.

Johnson's review reflected social snobbery: "Mr. Fleming dishes up his recipe with all the calculated accountancy of a Lyons Corner House." Raymond Chandler, a popular writer who admired Fleming, gave *Dr. No* a far more favorable review in the *Sunday Times*. Chandler proved eminently quotable: "Bond is what every man would like to be, and what every woman would like to have between her sheets." Like Fleming, Chandler's creation, the private detective Philip Marlowe, was a hardboiled hero.

Johnson was not alone. Already, Bernard Bergonzi, writing in the March 1958 issue of the *Twentieth Century*, had referred to "a strongly marked streak of voyeurism and sado-masochism" in the Bond novels and "the total lack of any ethical frame of reference," the latter a total misreading of the novels. The *Manchester Guardian*, a left-leaning newspaper, claimed that Fleming's work was "symptomatic of a decline in taste," which, again, reflected scant knowledge of the genre. In 1964, the West German conservative newspaper *Die Zeit*, referring to the film *From Russia, With Love*, called the Bond films "films close to Fascism." Similarly with both *Spiegel* and *Die Zeit* and their response to *Thunderball* in 1965: *Die Zeit* under the headline "The fine life and the speedy manslaughter." These, and other attacks, reflected disquiet about Bond's violence, sexual drive, and lifestyle, but also very much about his popularity, which was too great to ignore. Thus, in 1997, William Rees-Mogg, the pompous former editor of the *Times*, referred to Bond as "as a high technology killer, a sadistic womanizer and a pseudo sophisticate . . . a sinister bore."

Selective quotation played a role in the criticism of Bond and it is easy to see why. For example, in the Fleming short story "Quantum of Solace," Bond remarks that if he ever married he would marry an air hostess:

> It would be fine to have a pretty girl always tucking you up and bringing you drinks and hot meals and asking if you had everything you wanted. And they're always smiling and wanting to please. If I don't marry an air hostess, there'll be nothing for it but marry a Japanese. They seem to have the right ideas too.

Clear case for the prosecution: totally unreconstructed sexism plus a dose of racism. But read on: "Bond had no intention of marrying anyone. If he did, it would certainly not be an insipid slave. He only hoped to amuse or outrage the Governor into a discussion of some human topic." All too often selective quotations taken out of context have been employed to characterize Bond in a misleading fashion.

Critical themes were to be taken up by film reviewers, from *Dr. No* (1962) on. The film *Goldfinger* was attacked by Nina Hibbin (a frequent critic of Bond) in the Communist British newspaper the *Daily Worker*, as "one vast gigantic confidence trick to blind the audience to what is going on underneath." This, she claimed, was sadism, racialism, and "the glamorization of violence." Critics, and not only on the Left, frequently made such comments.

In comparison with Bond, the most commercially successful British films of 1959, 1962, and 1975, respectively—the smutty comedy *Carry on Nurse*, the Cliff Richard musical *The Young Ones*, and the soft-core *Confessions of a Window Cleaner*—have not attracted much critical or scholarly attention. The challenge of the marketplace to Establishment cultural politics, however, was serious, in other countries, such as West Germany, as well as in Britain. In 1963, the year after the first Bond film appeared, Sir

John Davis, managing director of the Rank Organisation, the owner of the powerful Odeon cinema chain, commented on the critically acclaimed real-life films of recent years, "I do feel that independent producers should take note of public demand and make films of entertainment value. The public has clearly shown that it does not want the dreary kitchen sink dramas," the last made obvious to Rank by the commercial failure of Lindsay Anderson's film *This Sporting Life* (1963). In *Comedians* (1975), a play by the left-wing playwright Trevor Griffiths, those comedians who remain true to their trainer's ideals, and believe that jokes should not exploit prejudices and sustain stereotypes, are rejected by the agent, who is "not looking for philosophers but for someone who sees what the people want and gives it to them."

This was a central aspect of the debate about morality of purpose that affected the arts throughout the period, a debate that influences the critical response to Bond. The debate was not simply an issue of how far art should have a moral purpose, but also over what this purpose should be. The left-wing artistic Establishment, which became increasingly influential from the 1960s, and in other countries, such as in West Germany, as well as in Britain, emphasized the need for the arts to engage with social issues, and subordinated both artist and individual members of the audience to group categories and environmental factors.

This was very much the antithesis of the Bond persona, for, however much he was a member of an organization, and far from a free spirit, he was also an individual whose adventures and role reflected the achievements of the hero, and the definition of the latter in terms of the self-reliant individual. Courage is a key virtue, and is seen to rest in the individual. Courage is a validator of personality, an indicator of moral worth, and a crucial means to success. For an artistic Establishment that had rejected heroes and to a degree embraced antiheroes and nonheroes, this validation was highly unwelcome. Furthermore, on the model of Fleming's wartime experiences, the courage that Bond displays is a result of commitment and duty, an acceptance of authority and yet, also a virtuous intransigence in the shape of a defiance of utilitarian calculations of action. At the same time, this intransigence is presented not as an easy choice but as one requiring great moral courage in the shape of fortitude. His character is more interesting than those of the interwar clubland heroes.

Debate about morality of purpose was, in turn, frequently linked to the issue of style. Much avant-garde culture asserted its higher purpose by presenting itself in terms of Modernism. In contrast, much popular art was Realist. To use the term to describe the generally improbable plots and limited characterization of Fleming or, indeed, other successful writers, such as Agatha Christie, may appear confusing, but they were realist in that they purported to represent the world as it was, using traditional means to do so, for example, not using dream sequences. Holmes had his "Baker Street Irregulars," while, in a deliberate use of class contrasts, Poirot interacted with lower-middle-class police officers such as Inspector Japp.

There were, of course, parallels between "highbrow" and "lowbrow" works. For example, both detective fiction and children's literature from the 1960s tackled issues that would have been generally regarded as inappropriate prior to that decade, and, by doing so, lessened the gap in content between them and more "highbrow" works. A wartime colleague and later friend of Fleming, Roald Dahl not only wrote the script for the Bond film *You Only Live Twice* (1967), but also produced surrealistic children's stories such as *James and the Giant Peach* (1961) and *Charlie and the Chocolate Factory* (1964), each of which had elements similar to Fleming's highly imaginative *Chitty Chitty Bang Bang* (1964). The last reflected the versatility of Fleming's imagination and his ability to reach for arresting characterization and dialogue. By the

1990s, Dahl's books were the most popular children's works in Britain.

Dahl was an experimenter, but the overwhelming characteristic of popular "lowbrow" works was a reluctance to experiment with form and style. This division also affected other arts, such as architecture, music, painting, and sculpture. Consequently, a pattern of contrast that was essentially set earlier in the century, with the impact of Modernism, remained important to the cultural life of the country and, indeed, the world. This pattern ensured that there were very differing understandings and experiences of culture and the arts.

This reminds us of the many contexts within which the Bond corpus was and is located, and the different forms of morality that culture serves to focus, from the morality of popularity in a democratized society, to that of supposed unchangeable values. The latter indeed have been under considerable pressure, and this has been reflected in the arts. The decline of the authority of the churches was related to the current of social change associated with the 1960s, although it was not confined to them. It is unsurprising, as well as striking, how negligible a role religion or the religious plays in the Bond stories or in the visual backgrounds of the films. Fake religion is criticized in the cases of voodoo (*Live and Let Die*) and television evangelism (*Licence to Kill*), but the general approach is distant. Some critics attacked the hedonism and self-centeredness of the permissive society, evinced in Bond films in sexual ease and product placement, but the impact of such attacks was limited. Campaigners against pornography and changing public standards, for example, Lord Longford and Mary Whitehouse, were cold-shouldered or lampooned by the media in Britain, and did not succeed in winning government support; the same was the case in the United States. In the 1980s and early 1990s, there were attempts in Britain, and even more in the United States, as part of the "culture wars" of the period, to reverse the libertarian trend, with talk of "family values," "back to basics," and the equivalents, but the movement had scant success.

Even its political sponsors in Britain, the Conservative governments of 1979 to 1997, made only a limited effort. Margaret Thatcher, prime minister from 1979 to 1990, attacked what she called the "progressive consensus," and told the *Times* on October 10, 1987, that children "needed to be taught to respect traditional moral values," but the liberal legislation of the 1960s was not reversed. Indeed, under Labour from 1997, there was further liberalization and libertarianism in sexual matters. In 2000, the British Board of Film Classification passed "hardcore" films for viewers aged eighteen and over. In Bond there was a move to "family friendly" with Moore, and to "family values," at least insofar as Bond became less hedonistic with Timothy Dalton and Pierce Brosnan, whereas, in contrast to "family friendly," however defined, Craig's Bond was edgy. The last was due more to the change of the audience's taste than to an attempt to return to Fleming's roots, although, as was usually the case, the latter factor was cited.

The media captured a sense of social and cultural fluidity in Britain. Television was more successful in setting the tone of British society than more historic institutions, such as the established churches. The latter, nevertheless, responded. In 1995, the General Synod of the Church of England abandoned the phrase "living in sin." Television encouraged a permissiveness in language and behavior by making such conduct appear normal. Indeed, by the mid-1990s, most British television and radio "soaps" seemed to have their quota of one-parent families, abused children, and sympathetically presented homosexuals.

This was a form of realism that, by contrast, underlined what, alongside the psychological insights of the Bond corpus, was its marked escapism, and its very conditional liberalism. Homosexuality was not the character of the hero, far from it; and nor was there any concession in the shape of bisexuality. Sexuality was crucial not only to the appeal of the Bond corpus, but also to Fleming's strong logic for the character he had created. This approach to homosexuality was very much the morality of his youth, which was still powerful in the 1950s. In 1960, indeed, the House of Commons rejected the recommendations of the Wolfenden Commission for the liberalization of the laws on homosexuality, which made homosexual acts between consenting adults criminal. In *Thunderball*, Blofeld was described as asexual: "he didn't smoke or drink and he had never been known to sleep with a member of either sex. He didn't even eat very much."

This was also a period in which the British secret services were being compromised. The defections to the Soviet Union of Guy Burgess and Donald Maclean in 1951, the arrest of George Blake in 1961, and the defection of Kim Philby in 1963, among other prominent cases, were scandals of incompetence and dishonesty, of traitors within and failures without. Intelligence scandals in the 1950s and 1960s contributed to a sense that the establishment as well as the government had failed. These scandals left few direct echoes in either the Bond novels or the films, although there was a discussion at the start of the novel *From Russia, With Love* about the problem of traitors, which sees Bond advocating the recruitment of homosexuals in order to hunt homosexual spies, which is instructive of Fleming's approach given the law at the time, which prohibited homosexual acts between consenting adults. Yet the general approach to homosexuals in the Bond corpus is pretty hostile. Thus, in a Miami restaurant in *Goldfinger*, the manager is described as "a pansified Italian." As a reminder of differing values, Bond accepts hospitality in Miami at the Floridiana, a hotel that he is told would not accept Jews, which, indeed, was the pattern of many American clubs and hotels at the time.

In the stories and films, there were very few problematic British agents. They were all either good or bad. The idea of a gray agent whose loyalty was not sure, even at the end, was not typical Bond. The closest were the likable rogue criminals, as in *On Her Majesty's Secret Service*, *GoldenEye*, and *The World Is Not Enough*, none of whom were British.

Intelligence scandals were an important context, both in implicit general terms, for the emphasis on automatically loyal service, and, more specifically, for the theme of ostentatious masculinity that was such an obvious feature of the Bond persona. This can be traced to Fleming's sense of heroism and his view of the likely readership, but was also a rejection of the ambiguity that Fleming saw in homosexuality. The homosexual traitor Burgess, an Old Etonian slightly younger than Fleming, was thus the antithesis of Bond. The distance from homosexuality has been maintained in the films, in which, from *Dr. No* to *Spectre*, Bond had sexual relations with fifty-eight women. The films are not really buddy movies, although Felix Leiter was briefly played in that role. The buddy quality was most pronounced not with Leiter but with female agents who were active partners, as in *Licence to Kill* and *Tomorrow Never Dies*.

In turn, Bond's sexual desire, like his repeated association with consumer goods, a theme amply taken forward from novels to films, was validated by his role and heroism. Furthermore, his desires are depicted as normal, not insatiable. Bond's attitude to women was presented as benign, not least in comparison to that of the villains. Thus, in *Goldfinger* Bond is revolted by reading a passage in a SMERSH manual: "'A drunken woman can also usually be handled by using the thumb and forefinger to grab the lower lip. By pinching hard and twisting, as the pull is made, the woman will come along.'" Bond's attitude also frequently led to crucial positive developments in the plots as "bad girls" were turned by him to good. This underlined the role of Bond's individualism. In particular at the end of *Goldfinger*, Bond wins over the lesbian Pussy Galore, who had "never met a man before." The book concluded as "His mouth came ruthlessly down on hers." Pussy Galore's change of attitude is crucial to the failure of Goldfinger's plan to gas Fort Knox's garrison, and thus to the plot—a process that was to recur in the film, but that can be seen as a weakness in the plot. The film does not bring up this lesbianism, other than elliptically, but has Bond achieving the same end.

The mechanistic megalomania of many of the villains and the sadistic evil of their agents are contrasted with Bond's sensuality. Goldfinger has a love of gold, a devouring greed, whereas Bond's sexual magnetism contrasts with the villain's physique and personality, a theme also seen with, for example, No, Blofeld, Drax, Stromberg, and others. There is much male fantasy here, but it is central to the image of Bond's sexuality that he gives, as well as receives, pleasure. This is an ability and desire that can be imagined of few of the male villains. Indeed, in the novel, Goldfinger's Korean henchmen are described as so sadistic in their use of prostitutes that some of the latter had died. A lack of engagement with women is also seen in such film portrayals as those of Dr. No and Blofeld.

Fleming's depiction of women who were not constrained or defined by the search for matrimony and motherhood, such as the vivid portrayal of Honeychilde Rider in *Dr. No*, contrasted with the women in the adventure stories of his childhood, for example, those of John Buchan (1875–1940). Many of these women were honorary chaps, or chaps with breasts, and small ones at that. Indeed, Richard Hannay's wife hunts and fishes with her husband. The emotional bond in those stories was that of Hannay and Sandy Arbuthnot. There was no comparable relationship between Bond and Leiter.

Instead of the depiction of women in earlier novels, the women in Fleming's works are presented as just as sexually active as

Bond. Thus, in the novel *Goldfinger*, but not the film, Jill Masterton accompanies Bond on the Silver Meteor train from Miami to New York. After their caviar sandwiches and best champagne, they had

> made long, slow love in the narrow berth [to] the rhythm of the giant diesels pounding out the miles. . . . She had woken him twice more in the night with soft demanding caresses, saying nothing, just reaching for his hard, lean body. The next day she had twice pulled down the roller blinds to shut out the hard light and had taken him by the hand and said, "Love me, James." . . . Neither had had regrets.

In *Thunderball*, Fleming refers to Dominetta Vital, Largo's mistress, as follows:

> "Whore," "tart," "prostitute" were not words Bond used about women unless they were professional streetwalkers or the inmates of a brothel. . . . This was an independent, a girl of authority and character. She might like the rich, gay life, but so far as Bond was concerned, that was the right kind of girl. She might sleep with men, obviously did, but it would be on her terms and not on theirs.

Fleming then pressed on to make a somewhat different point: "Women are often meticulous and safe drivers, but they are very seldom first-class. In general Bond regarded them as a mild hazard." At that stage, however, Dominetta Vital snubs Bond, leading him to call her (to himself) a bitch.

Bond's individualism in the novels frequently captures the dark side of the troubled Romantic hero; the theme repeatedly focuses on the sacrifices Bond has to endure. These include severe physical pain, particularly administered by captors, as in *Casino Royale* and *You Only Live Twice*; psychological pressure, not least the tension between introspection and duty, which leads to problems with mental health; loneliness, as in the close of the novel *Moonraker*; and the killing of his newly married wife, Tracy, at the end of *On Her Majesty's Secret Service*, both novel and film. In the pre-title sequence of the film *For Your Eyes Only*, Blofeld has Bond seized on his journey from the grave of his late wife.

Although the killing of Tracy is also a powerful episode on screen, there is no equivalent in the films to the general impression of forbearance and suffering created in the novels. Pain at the hands of the villains is far less to the fore than in the novels, notably in the novel *Casino Royale*; although, in *Die Another Day* (2002), Bond is depicted as being savagely tortured by the North Koreans and as showing a Christ-like forbearance. Indeed, the films, more generally, even the Dalton and Craig films, are more upbeat in mood as well as content, usually, and notably with the Moore films, offering a sense of humor and a lightness of tone that Fleming did not seek. In part, this contrast reflects a wider social current toward escapism and a corresponding devaluation of heroism as its costs are widely neglected. Escapism was particularly to the fore in the Moore films. The sense that film audiences want easy reassurance, indeed very easy viewing, is also a response to the need to produce a readily accessible global product.

Reassurance was the opposite of what was on offer in the novels. Instead, we are presented with a self-aware hero with a conscience. In addition, politics within Britain are discussed. In the novel *Casino Royale*, the reflective Bond, moreover, points to the mutability of political divisions: "If I'd been alive fifty years ago, the brand of Conservatism we have today would have been damn near called Communism and we should have been told to go and fight that." This was a clear reference to the Conservative government's willingness in the 1950s and early 1960s to maintain the welfare state created by their Labour predecessors, and to the sense of discontinuity that Conservatives of Fleming's generation felt as a consequence of the 1940s. This discontinuity and the resulting rejection by many Conservatives of the policies of the Conservative Party in the 1940s, 1950s, 1960s, and early 1970s, was to help fuel the rise of Thatcherism in the mid-1970s.

Yet, Bond's sense of values is not primarily political. Instead, his core virtue is repeatedly made a powerful counterpoint to his opponents' flaws: the foolish deceit, self-deceit, and overconfidence that are presented as integral to evil. These characteristics are epitomized with the repeated failure of villains who had seized Bond to dispatch him forthwith, and their doubly perverse desire to save him for a clever, cruel death after first showing glee in voicing their evil intentions toward both him and society as a whole, as in *Moonraker*. Satirists made fun of this process. More generally, there is a pattern to the plot in which the hubris and callousness of evil repeatedly provided opportunities for the bravery and integrity of Bond, in a counterpointing of intrigue and adventure.

The contrast in values was made clear in the novel *Casino Royale*. Vesper Lynd, Bond's assistant, with whom he has a romantic affair, commits suicide, admitting, in a letter to Bond, that she was a Soviet double agent, which accounts for Bond's travails in the novel. She explains that her boyfriend, a decorated ex-RAF Pole, had been a British agent, captured in Poland, tortured, and kept alive in order to force Vesper to cooperate. A continuation between World War II and the Cold War is clearly suggested here as elsewhere. It was a continuation in themes, plots, major characters, notably Blofeld and SPECTRE, and minor figures. For Fleming and Bond, the Soviets had replaced the Nazis, a worldview convincing to those who all along had opposed the Russian Revolution and had not been overly surprised by the Nazi-Soviet Pact in 1939–1941. In love with Bond, Vesper makes a virtuous act of self-sacrifice, an individual choice, renouncing Soviet control by killing herself.

This leads Bond to resolve to fight and destroy SMERSH, which he sees as the terror behind Soviet espionage. His closing phrase, "the bitch is dead now," probably the most striking in all the books, has sometimes been seen in a negative light. The phrase literally refers to Vesper, who, indeed, has betrayed him and is clearly a harshly unsympathetic response to her suicide. However, another reading of the phrase is possible. Bond had been discussing with René Mathis, his French secret service contact, the value of his role and had been expressing his uncertainty about staying in the service. In an approach that is somewhat different to that of the clubland heroes, and in a response to developing views, Bond says, "this country-right-or-wrong business is getting a little out-of-date." In contrast, the realization of SMERSH's exploitative and deadly methods leads, instead, to the end of Bond's doubts and, in this sense, the bitch is indeed dead.

The juxtapositions of hero and villain provide opportunities to underline the virtues of the former. In *Moonraker* (1955), the third novel, Fleming depicted Bond's world and its rationale in detail. In particular, this novel very much spoke to current anxieties in terms of nuclear warfare. Linked to this, far from the exoticism of the two previous novels, the story was very much one set in Britain. All the action took place in the small, tightly controlled world of London and nearby Kent. Exact locations were described at length. This was a world far distant from the subsequent rootlessness of the film (1979), which was set in California, Venice, Brazil, and outer space. Moreover, the novel *Moonraker* was tightly and brilliantly linked to the timetable of the rocket's launch, and the entire novel took place from a Monday to a Friday, with the chapter organization in terms of the passing days.

As in other novels, Fleming went into considerable detail to make the story more vital. The specifics of the rocket's design and motive system, and of the tracking and planning mechanisms, were described in detail. So also with the club Blades and with the card game between Drax and Bond, in which the cheater is brilliantly out-cheated and the extraordinary process fully explained in a lengthy but gripping passage that is of interest even to most non–card players, and certainly to me. This was a novel set where Bond lived. Indeed, in 1953, Fleming had bought a townhouse in Victoria Square, London, and he also had a house in Kent, a county where he regularly played golf and was to die. In *Goldfinger*, Blades is also a place where the villain plays cards, although the key card game is in Miami.

In terms of links between the novels, the life and character of Bond is depicted in *Moonraker* with details of his salary and life that are relevant for all the novels. Bond earned £1,500 annually pre-tax, the salary of a Principal Officer in the Civil Service, and, on top of that, his investments yielded him an additional £1,000 after tax. Thus, half his income came from private means, an aspect of the hero as an independent man of property, in this case shares. On £2,000 net, Bond could live very well, not least, as explained, as his costs were covered when he was on a mission.

Bond's personality and habits were described at length in *Moonraker*. Only two or three times a year did he have a mission requiring his 007 talents. The rest of the time, he is presented as having the duties of an easy-going senior civil servant. These are shown as elastic office hours from around 10:00 a.m. to 6:00 p.m., and in some of the novels he is processing files. For his spare time, Bond took no holidays, spent the evenings playing cards or "making love, with rather cold passion, to one of three similarly disposed married women," a relaxed mention of adultery, and weekends playing golf for high stakes. Lunch was generally in the officers' canteen. The lunch described has Bond tackle "a grilled sole, a large mixed salad with his own dressing laced with mustard, some Brie cheese and toast, and half a carafe of white Bordeaux," ending up with two cups of black coffee. This is a Fleming meal. Similarly, Holmes often has little or no work to do, and therefore can enjoy his pastimes. Neither man is really appreciated by the higher authorities.

Sir Hugo Drax, the villain in *Moonraker*, is a fake hero, a national savior who is really a Nazi in league with the Soviets. Behavior is a key indicator for Fleming, a reminder that, in popular fiction, outside conduct was a crucial sign of inside virtues: manners showeth the man. The social positioning of this identification was very different to that offered in most modern fiction. Drax is a social outsider, "a bullying, boorish, loud-mouth vulgarian," who sweated "rather freely," bit his nails, and, crucially, cheated at cards. He is also a "public hero," because of his construction of a rocket for Britain. This was not the politics of the "Angry Young Men" at this stage.

Fleming's approach might imply a criticism of mass society and its heroes, which may seem ironic in light of the subsequent mass popularity of Bond. The plot revealed how misguided the public could be, but also how vulnerable the Establishment was to new men, for Drax is new money, which was very much not a source of virtue in most eighteenth-, nineteenth-, and early-twentieth-century fiction. However, in the 1980s, in a very different context and tone, new money was to be treated very differently under the Thatcher government, which welcomed it. It is in accordance with more traditional values that, throughout *Moonraker*, Drax's conduct is contrasted with the true hero, Bond. Drax is repeatedly revealed as callous, cruel, and arrogant, as well as a perversion of gentility: "To me a gentleman is just someone I can take advantage of." Bond, in contrast, is presented as a gentleman, notably so in his treatment of Gala Brand, the heroine in the novel, in particular in his not taking advantage of her. The gentleman defeats the savage in the end.

The value of gentlemen was emphasized anew in *From Russia, With Love* (1957), probably the most fluent of the Bond novels, and one that was a great commercial success. It was also to be named by Kennedy in *Life Magazine* in March 1961 as one of his ten favorite books. In *From Russia, With Love*, there was a conscious emphasis on individual quality, which clashes with current notions of value:

> [Bond] reflected briefly on the way the Russians ran their centres—with all the money and equipment in the world, while the [British] Secret Service put against them a handful of adventurous, underpaid men. . . . Yet Kerim had the run of Turkey. Perhaps, after all, the right man was better than the right machine.

Earlier in the novel, and setting the scene, the fictional General Vozdvishensky of SMERSH is shown praising the British agents for their ability, professionalism, and honesty: despite paltry pay, they had achieved success, due in part, he suggests, to them being devoted agents who served because of their love of adventure. The enemy therefore values Bond. In the novel *Goldfinger* (1959), Bond reflects that he was up against "one of the greatest conspirators of all time. . . . How often in his profession had it been the same—the tiny acorn of coincidence that soared into the mighty oak whose branches darkened the sky. And now, once again, he was setting out to bring the dreadful growth down 'With what? A bag of golf clubs.'" This is very much a theme from the age of "clubland heroes." No longer the leader in technology, Britain had to rely on its wits and bravery, a theme also seen in war films. The honor of the hero is presented as more significant than the professionalism of the many and the organizations of bureaucracies. This theme was translated into the films. Indeed, although not in *Moonraker*, there could be a feeling of not being appreciated by the country and its leadership.

By personalizing the world of adventure, Fleming provided not only narrative structure but also a moral dimension, in which the identity of virtue was clear once the usual puzzle stage of the mystery had been solved; clear not least because the villains characteristically explained their manic plans with a callous self-confidence to the temporarily captured Bond. The arrogance and hubris of these villains were abundantly clear in these grandiloquent confessions. Those opposed to Britain, and thus civilization, were crooks, spiritually bankrupt, and morally without bearing. The conflation of crime and espionage focused on sinister individuals, and their personal failures condemned their cause and helped ensure their failure.

This theme of the resolute hero is still popular today despite many attempts to debunk or belittle heroism. Instead, the presentation of heroism very much answers to a deep need, as shown also by the potent and central role of heroism in the mythic fiction and films that have been so popular in recent years.

Reflective of a military mind-set, there was also an emphasis in the Bond novels on the need for firmness, a clarity in action matched to a certainty of purpose. Softness toward opponents is seen as a mistake because it rests on a misreading of the Soviets. In *From Russia, With Love*, Kerim Bey, the likable head of the British station in Istanbul, justifies killing Soviet agents, "They are hard people. With them, what you don't get from strength, you won't get from mercy. They are all the same, the Russians. I wish your government would realize it and be strong with them." Bond agrees, saying that the Russians "simply don't understand the carrot. Only the stick has any effect." Written the year after the very bloody Soviet suppression of the Hungarian reform movement in 1956, this expression of doubt would have appeared reasonable to many of Fleming's readers. The possibilities of better West-East relations that appeared in prospect after the death of Joseph Stalin in 1953, and that the British government had pursued, were now greatly shadowed. Indeed, the late 1950s were years of concern in the United States about a supposed "missile gap" with the Soviet Union.

The nature of the Soviet system was presented in *From Russia, With Love* in a particularly unattractive form with Colonel Rosa Klebb, Fleming's first female villain. Portrayed as a sadistic lesbian, she was another aspect of Fleming's linkage of homosexuality with dangerous leanings. Again, Fleming coined his experiences. Klebb was based on a Colonel Rybkin he had written about in the *Sunday Times* while Fleming had visited Istanbul for an Interpol conference in 1955. He had traveled home by the Orient Express, although he disliked it as it lacked a restaurant car. The last was crucial for the style of train travel and also to cope with boredom. In the film, the scene in the restaurant car was very important. In his own copy of the book, Fleming recorded:

> The Russian background comes mostly from a Soviet refugee spy called Tokaev—alias Tokati—an excellent man. I was in Istanbul for the *Sunday Times*. . . . The gypsies will stage a fight between girls for a small sum. The Orient Express is a dull, dirty train. I took great trouble over this book.

The theme of necessary firmness toward opponents is very much one taken throughout the novels. The puzzle consists of identifying Britain's opponents and understanding their purposes rather than determining what to do with them. Indeed, one obvious contrast between the real world and that of Bond, at least until the film *Spectre* (2015), is that Bond is not held politically or legally responsible for his actions. This may help to explain the appeal of the films to modern audiences. They are not located in the world of public enquiries, accountability, and health and safety. This contrast with the bureaucratic reality of organized life, however, is one that has become more extraordinary with the years, although that is true, more generally, of adventure series.

Kerim Bey is an example of the good foreigner, but, in general, there is a national bias in the depiction of virtue that reflects British assumptions and values that are long gone from public culture. Deracination is a particular target of Fleming, while immigration is deplored. This is not only true of Britain, but also of the United States and other countries. In "From a View to a Kill," a Bond short story published in 1960, which was based on an unsuccessful television script for CBS, there is a jaundiced view of Paris and the French. This perspective is not necessary to the story, but brings together ethnic stereotyping and the crisis of France under the Fourth Republic, a France defeated by left-wing anti-colonial nationalists in Indochina and under pressure in Algeria. In a warning to London, Paris is presented as a city that has sold its heart to tourists and foreigners, "You could see it in the people's eyes—sullen, envious, ashamed," and French female beauty deceives:

> On closer examination she would . . . have the heavy, dank, wide-pored skin of the bourgeois French. The blond hair under the rakish velvet beret would be brown at the roots. . . . The peppermint on the breath would not conceal the midday garlic. The alluring figure would be intricately scaffolded with wire plus rubber.

In contrast, the France on display in the early part of the film *A View to a Kill* (1985), the France of Paris and the chateau (palace) of Chantilly, was very different; with the Paris of the Eiffel Tower and the River Seine then serving as an elegant setting for danger, and without any reflections on the French. By then, however, as we come to in the discussion of the films, only the titles remained from Fleming's writing. Bond himself had long changed. It was not only social values that had been transformed.

3

THE LATER NOVELS

It is indeed kind of you to send James Bond some of your beautiful new bottles of the Blanc de Blancs for '53, which I believe to be superb.

Unfortunately, James Bond is at present in Japan where the poor fellow will have nothing to drink but sake.

I shall try and play fair with him, but it may well be that by the time he returns he will find nothing but the empty bottles.

But these are so handsome that he can certainly have them converted into lamps!

As Fleming's letter of April 9, 1963, to the champagne producer Claude Taittinger showed, he was well able to distance himself from Bond. This distance from his creation was captured in an interview published in *The New Yorker* on April 21, 1962. He dismissed his books as having "no social significance," and his own role as the author: "it's a terrible indictment of my own character—they are so adolescent." Fleming added,

When I wrote the first book in 1953 I wanted Bond to be an extremely dull, uninteresting man to whom things happened; I wanted him to be a blunt instrument. One of the bibles of my youth was *Birds of the West Indies* by James Bond, a well-known ornithologist, and when I was casting about for a name

for my protagonist I thought, My God, that's the dullest name
I've ever heard, so I appropriated it.

The use of a dull and passive name was good for a secret agent.
Self-deprecatory in the established way, the interview reflected
Fleming's authorial distance from his creation, but also the
marked degree of ennui in his later years. This ennui could entail
despair, the despair of a Briton of his class and generation seeing
the empire disappear, the country decline, social indicators discarded, and past values dismissed. In Fleming's case, there was
also the ennui that was linked to his growing ill health, as well as
the disillusionment stemming from the well-known affair that,
from 1956, Ann, his wife, the patron of a notable Conservative
salon group, had with Hugh Gaitskell, the leader of the Labour
Party. From 1955, Fleming, of course, had his own lover, and his
own commitment to the West Indies was in part linked to his sex
life.

The marked implausibility of the three SPECTRE novels,
Thunderball (1961), *On Her Majesty's Secret Service* (1963), and
You Only Live Twice (1964), was an aspect of the change in
Fleming and Bond. Well written and paced, *Thunderball*, the
novelization of a film script that had not yet been filmed, repre-
sented a striking new departure with the introduction of SPEC-
TRE (the Special Executive for Counterintelligence, Terrorism,
Revenge, and Extortion), which is described in detail and pre-
sented as evil unconstrained by ideology, the latter very different
to SMERSH (SMERt' SHpionam—Death to Spies).

The structure of SPECTRE's governing council reveals that
the twenty members include three members of the Gestapo,
Fleming's benchmark for evil, just as Blofeld had worked for the
Abwehr, the German military intelligence agency. The chief vil-
lain Bond encounters is described as having "the ruthlessness of a
Himmler." The council meeting that is discussed shows that
SPECTRE has recovered Himmler's jewels from the Mondsee,

where they had been hidden, and disposed of them in Beirut. The dramatic buildup in the council meeting, and thus to the story, is linked to the kidnapping and ransoming of the daughter of an American gangster who had been deflowered while a captive being held for ransom. The asexual Blofeld declares that sexual experience might be beneficial, very much a Fleming view, and that SPECTRE is not concerned with morality; but he also makes it clear that discipline is crucial. As a consequence, the guilty party, SPECTRE No. 12, Pierre Borraud, is electrocuted with 3,000 volts at the council meeting. This was an industrial fate that contrasted with the blinding administered at such a meeting in the film *Spectre* (2015); although, in the novel *Thunderball*, it is revealed that Blofeld had earlier killed two others at a council, the first with a needle fired from a compressed air pistol and the second by a garroting.

The introduction of SPECTRE in 1961 can be seen as a surrender to fantasy, occasioned in part by the decline of the British Empire and by Fleming's consequent lack of certainty about the country's position, a lack of certainty matching his more general despair as well as being a concession to the original film script on which the novel is based. With SPECTRE, there is a shift from the Soviet threat to a more film-friendly "ominous" danger, which adds greater drama. Britain is still presented in *Thunderball* as playing a major role, M declaring: "We've teamed up with the CIA to cover the world. Allen Dulles is putting every man he's got on to it and so am I," as if the two were equal. Dulles was director of the CIA from 1953 to 1961, when he had to resign after the failure of the Bay of Pigs attempt to overthrow Fidel Castro, the Cuban Communist dictator.

In the council meeting, SPECTRE discusses Plan Omega, its biggest project so far. Two atom bombs are to be seized from a British Villiers Vindicator experimental bomber when it is hijacked on a training flight. Britain had indeed been dropping nuclear bombs in weapons tests for several years. The hijacking is handled with detail, as is the construction of Largo's boat. SPEC-TRE demands £100 million in gold bullion for the return of the bombs. Britain and the United States decide not to pay up, but to defeat the challenge. The threat posed by the hijacking is also described in great detail, including the problems of tracking the bomber and the issues involved in detonating a nuclear bomb. M explains why he thinks the bomber has been taken to the Bahamas and why the bombs are designed for targets in the wealthier and more bomb-conscious United States, rather than in Britain. Bond himself is skeptical about SPECTRE, and more inclined to emphasize the threat from the Soviet Union: "I'd rather have had somewhere more interesting—the Iron Curtain beat for instance. . . . For my money this looks more like a Russian job. They get the experimental plane and the bombs . . . and throw dust in your eyes with all this SPECTRE ballyhoo."

Bond is given CIA support in the Bahamas, then still part of the empire and only gaining independence in 1973. Fleming had visited the Bahamas. The CIA support provides an opportunity for probing the unsettled nature of the Anglo-American relationship: Bond fears he will be sent "a muscle-bound ex-college man with a crew-cut and a desire to show up the incompetence of the British . . . to gain credit with his chief," a presentation presumably based on some of the Americans Fleming had met. In fact, Bond gets the helpful Leiter. In *Thunderball*, Bond is keen to borrow superior American technology and weaponry, including portable Geiger counters, while the *Manta*, an American atomic submarine, plays a role in helping thwart the villain. Its commander tells Bond, "These atomic weapons are just too damned dangerous. Why, any one of these little sandy cays around here could hold the whole of the United States to ransom—just with one of my missiles trained on Miami." This reflection pointed the way forward for the espionage/adventure novel, and for the Bond films.

There is a more profound reflection. How best to deal with the villain is a key problem—one that cuts to the quick of the problems of fighting within the law. Until the bombs are on board Largo's ship, there are no legal grounds for seizing him or it. In a passage that reflects Fleming's views, Bond complains that he is like a detective tailing a suspected murderer: "there's nothing the detective can do but follow the man and wait until he actually pulls the gun out of his pocket."

Thunderball also provides much detail on Bond, building upon the earlier accounts of him. There is no comparison with Bond to the discontinuities seen with the introduction of SPECTRE. For example, the Mark II Continental Bentley that Bond has is described in considerable detail, including the cost of the work in improving it to his specifications—the latter a mark of his individuality. Bond's response to the car is also covered in some detail: "Bond loved her more than all the women at present in his life rolled, if that were feasible, together." At the same time, it was, as ever, necessary to read on, rather than rely on a selective quotation: "But Bond refused to be owned by any car. A car, however splendid, was a means of locomotion."

Food was another type of locomotion. Bond rejects the improving diet at the health spa of Shrublands to which he is sent: "I need some proper food . . . make me your kind of scrambled eggs—four eggs. Four rashers of that American hickory-smoked bacon if we've got any left, hot buttered toast—your kind, not wholemeal—and a large pot of coffee, double strength. And bring in the drink tray. . . . Plenty of time to watch the calories when one gets to heaven." Bond also criticizes "the inflated bogosity of tourist hotel food." Bond has to choose Native Seafood Cocktail Suprême, followed by Tender Farm Chicken, while Leiter has Baltic Herring in Sour Cream followed by Chopped Tenderloin of Beef; and they conclude that it is just "badly cooked rubbish." Leiter thinks his beef is "bad hamburger."

Moving ahead, a valedictory tone, for Fleming and his world, was readily apparent in the description of a meeting with M in *On Her Majesty's Secret Service*. Bond greatly appreciated M's reminiscences about the Royal Navy, in which he had been an admiral. Fleming, who had served in the wartime navy, albeit in an essentially desk job, commented: "Perhaps it was all just the stuff of boys' adventure books, but it was all true and it was about a great Navy that was no more and a great breed of officers and seamen that would never be seen again." Indeed, Britain had had the largest navy in the world from the early 1690s to the latter stages of World War II. Fleming frequently made naval references and they would have resonated with his audience. Yet, the navy that had fought the war was literally being dismantled. Britain's last battleship, the HMS *Vanguard*, was scrapped in 1960; laid down in 1941 and commissioned in 1946, she was the largest battleship built for a European navy. Moreover, in rivalry with the army and air force, the Royal Navy had lost out in new defense expenditure. Indeed, successive heads of the navy had resigned in protest in 1946 and 1948.

The sense of loss in *On Her Majesty's Secret Service* focused on nobility of character and service, whereas in *You Only Live Twice* the message is very much that Britain itself is weakening on the world stage; this weakness is highly significant for the plot, both in terms of devices and with reference to tone. Already, in the short story "The Hildebrand Rarity," published in 1960, Milton Krest, a villainous American collector of rare species, and the name of a villain in *Licence to Kill* (1989), has treated Bond to an account of British inconsequence:

> "Nowadays," said Mr. Krest, "there were only three powers—America, Russia and China. That was the big poker game and no other country had either the chips or the cards to come into

it. Occasionally some pleasant little country . . . like England would be lent some money so that they could take a hand with the grown-ups. But that was just being polite like one sometimes had to be—to a chum in one's club who'd gone broke."

Bond finds this argument oversimplified and naïve, and recalls an aphorism about America lacking "a period of maturity." Nevertheless, Krest's words reflected the growing perception of Britain as weak and the willingness of people to mention this weakness. Decolonization by Britain was gathering pace and becoming the normal outcome for colonies. Moreover, the British intelligence system appeared heavily compromised. In December 1961, a KGB officer who defected to the United States revealed that a list of KGB agents in deep cover compiled by MI6 had reached the KGB. This led to an investigation of the head of MI5, Sir Roger Hollis, who was held responsible for a failure to thwart Soviet espionage, although he was cleared of being a traitor.

In this and other stories, Bond's style could barely conceal the diminished British political and military presence in Cold War confrontations. In the person of the wife-beating Krest—whose wife in fact murders him, and deservedly so—wealth and power became insensitivity and sadism, which was an unsettling account of what British weakness could lead to. The story is a highly moral one. Krest gets his comeuppance. He has the fish he is searching for, the "Hildebrand Rarity," crammed into his mouth, with its deadly spines caught inside his cheeks. His death and its consequences are described vividly. Krest is a villainous threat not only to those he met but also to the underwater world he plundered. In the story, which is set in the tropics, albeit in this case the Indian Ocean, not the Caribbean, Fleming indeed offers an attractive account of the latter, and notably of the reef: "A dozen varieties of butterfly and other reef-fish flirted among the rocks, and a small langouste quested toward Bond with its feelers. The head of a large green moray protruded from a hole, its half-open jaws showing the rows of needle teeth. Its golden eyes watched Bond carefully."

This was a deadly world with which Fleming was comfortable, and he gave that assurance to Bond.

The same year, "Quantum of Solace" offered another account of the tropics—in this case of a dinner party with the governor of the Bahamas. The story began with a clear account of Bond's wide-ranging dislikes:

> He was never comfortable sitting deep in soft cushions. He preferred to sit up in a solidly upholstered armed chair with his feet firmly on the ground. . . . Bond didn't like Nassau. Everyone was too rich. The winter visitors and the residents who had houses on the island talked of nothing but their money, their diseases and their servant problems. They didn't even gossip well. There was nothing to gossip about. The winter crowd were all too old to have love affairs and, like most rich people, too cautious to say anything malicious about their neighbours.

Humans are apparently far less interesting than fish, although the story reveals otherwise. A sense of passing is repeatedly present. In *The Spy Who Loved Me* (1962), Bond is part of "these old people" and the "Stone Age stuff" criticized by the heroine Vivienne Michel, a young Canadian. Ironically, the novel is written very arrestingly from her perspective—an approach that most readers did not like. The novel, however, displayed Fleming's impressive range and skill as a writer. Much of it was a "hard-edged" account of the "sentimental education" of a young woman, who is in many respects a victim, and Bond does not appear until much of the way through the story. His backstory in this plot is far less important than that of Vivienne, but focuses on his successfully thwarting SPECTRE's attempt, on behalf of the Soviets, to kill a Soviet defector with a specialty in nuclear submarines. In this attempt, SPECTRE employs a former Gestapo agent who is using local gangland support. The association is typical of Fleming's view of the convergence of evil and his interest in what had happened to ex-Nazis.

Having thwarted them, Bond is en route overland to Washington, only for his car to have a flat. This ensures that he ends up in the motel where Vivienne, the receptionist, is menaced with rape and murder as part of an insurance fraud on behalf of the owner, Mr. Sanguinetti, which is yet another instance of Fleming's suspicion of Italian Americans. Bond kills Slugsy and Horror, Sanguinetti's menacing thugs, and has sex with Vivienne before leaving, taking his "private jungle" with him. He is the hero as savior and is the sole attractive male in the life Vivienne had had hitherto.

The Spy Who Loved Me, Fleming's attempt at "kitchen sink" realism, was one of Fleming's best pieces and one of the best Bond novels. Most male reviewers hated the book, but the few women who reviewed it found it (or at least the first half, which dealt with Vivienne's backstory) sympathetic and realistic. With this novel, Fleming proved able to think his way into somebody completely different, which was a contrast to his frequent failure to create three-dimensional or sometimes even two-dimensional characters.

The morality of espionage, discussed briefly at the close of *The Spy Who Loved Me*, attracted Fleming's attention as part of a wider consideration of values. In the short story "The Living Daylights," originally published in 1962 as "The Berlin Escape," nuclear disarmament, then a popular cause on the Left, notably in Britain, is presented as weakening the West. Moreover, Sender, his escorting officer, threatens Bond for deliberately firing to hit the gun of a Soviet agent, and not at the agent, a beautiful woman. This episode plays a role in a key section of the 1987 film of the same name. Like many of the Bond stories, including the posthumously published "Octopussy" (1965), "The Living Daylights" presented Fleming with the opportunity to use his hero in order again to discuss his values. Set in Berlin, and very much part of the beat of the Cold War, Bond is shown as contemptuous of his orders and as disliking the conformity of officialdom.

Fleming knew that the wartime buccaneering of his own naval intelligence days, a system made necessary by the pressures of war, had long been replaced by a utilitarian bureaucracy, which, in the case of Britain, owed much to Labour's corporatism. As a result, in the novels, stoical duty and an almost disillusioned love of country become apparent as motivators, rather as they did for George Orwell. In a threatening world, Bond is necessary, even if his duty and his conscience are repeatedly shown as creating psychological tensions—tensions that lead him to a breakdown.

Thunderball had had the energy and interest of a new departure and creations, notably SPECTRE and Blofeld. However, the atmosphere in the later novels is far less positive and the writing and inventiveness less dynamic. In plot terms, this was not only because of Britain's decline, and Bond's psychological ill health, but also due to concern about the values of the organizational culture of British (and American) intelligence. This was seen in the clash of manner between Bond and the bankmanagerish American Colonel Schreiber in "From a View to a Kill" (1960). Schreiber is no Leiter. This approach is followed by the more pronounced emphasis on Bond's conscience and independence (and willingness to drink on duty), in rebelling against the bureaucratic Sender in "The Living Daylights" (1962), a story that was to appear in the collection *Octopussy* (1966). Both stories look toward the clashes with the utilitarian and humorless Ms in the films *Never Say Never Again* (1983), and (far less amusingly) *GoldenEye* (1995) and *Spectre* (2015).

By the early 1960s, Fleming was becoming depressed about Britain's decline, and *You Only Live Twice* (1964) contains a complaint about press and political intervention in the running of the Secret Service, which indeed had been hit by scandals, as well as containing praise for the notion of rule by an elite. The latter was instructive as the Conservatives, under another Old Etonian, Alec Douglas-Home, were to lose to Labour, under Gaitskell's successor, Harold Wilson, in the general election of 1964. Modern British society is castigated as a whole: its moral fiber has been sapped by the excessive power of the trade unions, leaving behind "a vacuous, aimless horde . . . whining at the weather and the declining fortunes of the country, and wallowing nostalgically in gossip about the doings of the Royal Family." In its defense, Bond argues that the country had been bled thin by the world wars, that welfare-state politics made the people expect too much for free, that decolonization had been overly speedy (a charge that indeed can be defended), and that the politicians were incompetent; but "we still climb Everest and beat plenty of the world at plenty of sports and win Nobel Prizes." The villain Blofeld believes that England is sick, and that "hastening the sickness to the brink of death" would inspire a renewed national effort. He himself has created in Japan "a sort of Disneyland of Death," an inappropriate comparison that was possibly most pertinent for an American audience.

You Only Live Twice reflected Fleming's increasing melancholia about Britain, with Bond mirroring the author's moods and indeed a more general perception of national weakness. Britain is in decline, the Americans are refusing to pass on information, in part because they treat the Pacific as a "private preserve," and, therefore, the British seek intelligence information from Japan, and have to earn it by Bond's use on a mission for specifically Japanese ends. In his rapid 1959 tour to Hong Kong, Macao, and Tokyo, reporting for the *Sunday Times*, Fleming had noted Britain's greatly lessened influence in East Asia and the Pacific.

That is not the sum total of British weakness, however. In the book, a Soviet scheme to use nuclear blackmail to force the removal of American bases from Britain and British nuclear disarmament is thwarted by Kennedy's willingness to threaten nuclear war—a step taken as a result of British intelligence information. The implication is clear that this is a description of a real episode, and that Britain's position is threatened. Visiting Washington in early 1960, Fleming met Kennedy, then a Massachusetts senator; he asked Fleming for his advice about Fidel Castro, who had gained control of Cuba at the start of 1959 and was rapidly moving the country leftward.

You Only Live Twice looks back to the issue of nuclear power in *Moonraker* (1955), and reflects the role of nuclear confrontation in the Cuban missile crisis of 1962 between the United States and the Soviet Union, in which Britain had not played a significant role, in part because the American missiles based there were not mentioned often. However, as America's leading ally, Britain would have been involved in any war that America fought with the Soviet Union.

In this crisis there was mention of possibilities seen in *Dr. No*. In a meeting on August 10, 1962, with Secretary of State Dean Rusk, John McCone, director of the Central Intelligence Agency, voiced the suspicion that the Soviet Union could disrupt American missile flights from Cape Canaveral: "that this could be electronic equipment for use against Canaveral and/or military equipment including medium-range ballistic missiles." The source was most likely a Cuban refugee. On August 31, 1962, Senator Kenneth Keating told the Senate,

> Castro has virtually handed the Communists a gigantic monkey-wrench that can be turned right through the middle of our entire space effort, that can endanger the lives of our astronauts, and that can critically slow down vital defense developments. It is time for the people of this country and of this hemisphere to have the truth, the whole truth, about what Castro and his Soviet cohorts are up to . . . the Soviets might be constructing missile bases, but he focused on potential radio interference with the Cape Canaveral space program.

In *You Only Live Twice* the need for revival and national effort was linked to a contrast, made or implied, between the "people" in Britain (essentially good but threatened by bad politics) and the polity (in decline, corrupt, incompetent, and requiring saving by an elite). This approach reflected the growing mental exhaustion of the increasingly ill and demoralized Fleming, and it did not offer much for the future. This approach also tied in with the idea of Bond as a dutiful servant of a cause in which a combination of the morality of the mission, the integrity of the agent, and the solidity of the intelligence agency compensated for defects elsewhere, including that of the public being served. This theme can be seen repeatedly in the novels of the clubland heroes.

You Only Live Twice had near the very end an obituary for Bond that offered a comment on Fleming's novels. They were presented as based on real adventures:

> The inevitable publicity, particularly in the foreign press, accorded some of these adventures, made him, much against his will, something of a public figure, with the inevitable result that a series of popular books came to be written around him by a personal friend and former colleague of James Bond. If the quality of these books, or their degree of veracity, had been any higher, the author would certainly have been prosecuted under the Official Secrets Act. It is a measure of the disdain in which these fictions are held at the Ministry, that action has not yet—I emphasize the qualification—been taken against the author and publisher of these high-flown and romanticized caricatures of episodes in the career of an outstanding public servant.

There was also an exhausted tone for the villain, Blofeld: "A year earlier, the usual quiet tones that Bond remembered so well would never have cracked into that lunatic, Hitler scream. And the coolness, the supreme confidence that had always lain behind his planning? Much of that seemed to have seeped away." The comparison was to be repeated, with the phrase "the Hitlerian scream," as well as the cruelty of torture by Japanese guards, and Irma Bunt's sadistic commitment to Blofeld's cause.

The confrontation between Bond and Blofeld enabled both to criticize the other. Blofeld has a low view of Bond, not vindicated by Fleming's characterization of him: "You are a common thug, a blunt instrument wielded by dolts in high places. Having done what you are told to do, out of some mistaken idea of duty or patriotism, you satisfy your brutish instincts with alcohol, nicotine and sex while wanting to be dispatched on the next misbegotten foray." This ironically was the theme of the literary critics, such as Paul Johnson in 1958. Blofeld himself confesses to a "certain lassitude of mind." He also seeks to justify himself, presenting the thwarted Operation Thunderball as a warning about the need for serious disarmament talks so that atomic weapons do not get into dangerous hands. It is unclear how far this remark is distanced by being given to a villain. The story rambles at times, and reflected Fleming's continued problem with writing effective dialogue. Based on a story he used to tell his young son, *Chitty Chitty Bang Bang* was a more satisfying publication of 1964. Written from 1961, it was about an adventurous family and their magical flying and sailing car.

However, the 500 cigarettes a week, vodka martinis, and scrambled eggs Fleming consumed were all having a toll. He had Bond follow the same diet, but also claimed that, due to his hazardous career, Bond would not live for long. The Cecil Beaton photograph showed Fleming smoking before an array of bottles, and he was usually seen with a cigarette. He appeared at ease, and sometimes was, but the impact of his lifestyle was very different. In April 1961, Fleming had a heart attack, possibly due to being sued by Kevin McClory and Jack Whittingham, the cowriters of the screen treatment that he had turned into *Thunderball*. They claimed he had stolen the plot.

Success in getting the novels filmed, however, gave the exhausted Fleming more interest. In 1963, he went along to Istanbul while *From Russia, With Love* was being filmed—a trip he could charge against tax—and stayed there with the film's director, Terence Young. Yet, there was an element of melancholia: Fleming became friends with Pedro Armendariz, the actor playing Kerim Bey, who, it turned out, had advanced cancer. They discussed the prospect of committing suicide in such circumstances, and, indeed, Pedro did so soon after his work was over. Fleming complained that the fight between the two gypsy women was less explicit than in his novel, but Young had to be conscious of the censors.

A disillusioned and tired Fleming died of a heart attack on August 12, 1964, leaving over £300,000, a substantial sum for those days. Published posthumously, *The Man with the Golden Gun* (1965) warned about links between the KGB, the Mafia, Black Power, terrorism, and drugs. The novel linked the Soviet Union, Cuba, drugs, and subversion, both in the West Indies and more widely, including "the big black uprising." However, skepticism was expressed about the likely success of American pressure on Castro: "If the Americans once let up on their propaganda and needling and so forth, perhaps even make a friendly gesture or two, all the steam'll go out of the little man." Fleming captured Castro's dependence on a sense of siege, but not the vigor of Castro's secret police. This was a somewhat exhausted novel, and it depicted Bond in that light. Because Britain was no longer the imperial power in Jamaica, Bond does not receive due recognition for his success.

Already, however, at the time of his death, Fleming had sold about thirty million books, and had been presented nine times with the Golden Pen award for sales of over one million paperback copies of individual books. Moreover, a degree of creativity was suggested by the other stories that followed posthumously, the collection *Octopussy* being published in 1966. It contained three short stories, the title one copyrighted in 1965. This was a brilliant portrayal of character, notably of Dexter Smythe, a former Royal Marine in a "very special task force," who "had arrived at the frontier of the death-wish" and was drinking and smoking in defiance of the doctor and of warning heart attacks. A brandy breakfast was his routine at 10:30 a.m. In a portrayal in which Fleming was not absent, Smythe engaged more with the underwater marine life off Jamaica than with the white population on Jamaica.

Smythe is visited by Bond, and thereby recalled to his troubled past. This relates to the last stage of the war, meaning, of course, World War II. Having found the location of a Nazi gold haul in 1945, Smythe had murdered Oberhauser, the German alpine guide he had used to reach the location, and seized the gold. Smythe had then emigrated to Jamaica, and offered an account of the contrast with Britain that presumably reflected Fleming's view:

> their life was one endless round of parties . . . it was paradise all right, while, in their homeland, people munched their spam, fiddled in the black market, cursed the government and suffered the worst winter weather for thirty years.

Although popular in Hawai'i, Spam in Britain was a particularly revolting form of processed meat that I remember from school lunches. Bond tracks Smythe down on behalf of MI6 and swiftly makes it clear that there is also a personal dimension—one that gives the story bite: "It just happened that Oberhauser was a friend of mine. He taught me to ski before the war, when I was in my teens. . . . He was something of a father to me at a time when I happened to need one." Oberhauser was to be deployed anew in the complex psychodrama of the film *Spectre* (2015) as part of Bond's backstory. Instead of going for trial, Smythe benefits from

Bond's deliberate decision to give him a choice about the outcome. Smythe goes for a swim, only to be bitten by the poisonous scorpion fish and then eaten alive by the octopus he had been feeding. Underwater marine life as deadly as well as fascinating emerges yet again as both description and plot device.

After Fleming, the novels continued. As a character, Bond could not be effectively copyrighted, and the best way to deal with the threat of imitations was for Glidrose, which owned the Bond publishing rights, to commission a sequel. The first was *Colonel Sun* (1968). It was dedicated to Fleming by the avid Bond fan and major novelist Kingsley Amis, writing under the pseudonym Robert Markham. In this novel, the Chinese were the villains, seeking to exploit Cold War hostilities between Britain and the Soviet Union to their own ends. Amis had offered suggestions for finishing off *The Man with the Golden Gun* when Fleming died and in 1965 had published *The James Bond Dossier*.

Amis took up Fleming's themes, as did later successors. At the end of *Colonel Sun*, Ariadne Alexandrou, the heroine, says to Bond about their work, "People think it must be wonderful and free and everything. But we're not free, are we?" "No," said Bond again, "We're prisoners. But let's enjoy our captivity while we can." Change threatened public virtue, however, and Amis echoed the reaction against the modern world, or at least features of it (there was and is a crucial difference), seen in Fleming's account of Paris in "From a View to a Kill" (cited at the end of the previous chapter), or his presentation of Istanbul, a city he had visited for the *Sunday Times*, in *From Russia, With Love* (1957):

> The old European section of Istanbul glittered at the end of the broad half-mile of bridge with the slim minarets lancing up into the sky and the domes of the mosques, crouching at their feet, looking like big firm breasts. It should have been the Arabian Nights, but to Bond, seeing it first above the tops of trams and above the great scars of modern advertising along

the river frontage, it seemed a once beautiful theatre-set that modern Turkey had thrown aside in favour of the steel and concrete flat-iron of the Istanbul-Hilton Hotel, blankly glittering behind him on the heights of Pera.

That was very much Fleming writing, and helped explain his choice of the architect of London Modernism for the naming of his villain Goldfinger. To Amis, in *Colonel Sun*, the world had become a scene depicting mediocrity and tastelessness, and a product of vulgarity as opposed to class. Soon after the opening of the book, Bond drives across a part of England, in this case Berkshire, and notes "the ugly rash of modern housing . . . the inevitable TV aerial sprouting from every roof." Overhead, planeloads of tourists set forth from Heathrow for destinations as far as Spain and Portugal, exporting their "fish-and-chip culture." Amis continued, "But it was churlish to resent all this and the rising wage levels that made it possible. Forget it." Nevertheless, alongside the tone, it was the bitter criticism that struck: more means worse, a characteristic of Amis's dyspeptic and conservative tone in his writing as a whole. Popular culture and prosperity are held up for criticism.

The same passage also identified Bond with a sense of true nature, a repeated theme in conservative ideas of national identity. For example, the speeches of the Conservative leader of 1923–1937, Stanley Baldwin, were littered with respectful and potent eulogies to the English countryside and the sons of the soil, a political aspect of a pastoralism that has been incessantly rejected from the 1960s, by repeated attempts to emphasize the appeal of urban identities. Bond drives past productive farms and ancient forests that would long stand "as memorials of what England had once been," before mass urbanization. This is very similar to Fleming's praise of rural Kent in *Moonraker*.

Later in *Colonel Sun*, in the international atmosphere of Constitution Square in the center of Athens, Bond reflects on a similar theme, although it is developed in a surprising fashion:

> What Ariadne Alexandrou had said about the decreasing Greekness of Greece came to Bond's mind. In thirty years, he reflected, perhaps sooner, there would be one vast undifferentiated culture . . . stretching from Los Angeles to Jerusalem; possibly, by then, as far as Calcutta. . . . Where there had been Americans and British and French and Italians and Greeks and the rest, there would be only citizens of the West, uniformly affluent, uniformly ridden by guilt and neurosis, uniformly alcoholic and suicidal, uniformly everything. But was that prospect hopelessly bad? Bond asked himself. Even at the worst, not as bad as all that was offered by the East, where conformity did not simply arise as if by accident, but was consciously imposed to the hilt by the unopposed power of the State.

This was the consolation of a depressive, which Amis, like Fleming, had indeed become. Both men also drank and smoked heavily. The notion of an "End of History," of a uniform, deracinated, decultured West located in 1998, was presented not as triumph, but as a source of despair, only for the consolation to be offered that the alternative was even worse, which was certainly a definition of the situation in 1998. This, however, was a deeply pessimistic, skeptical conservatism directed against globalization. There was no sense of national survival and success, nor of the possible triumph of Western values or of capitalism, both of which had mistakenly appeared possible in the 1990s. Bond's villains themselves expose great wealth as morally corrosive and as the source or means of dangerous hubris. In Amis's view, capitalism, like Communism, is an enemy of identity. This, indeed, was a key element of the British rejection of the European Union seen with the Brexit victory in 2016. Moreover, nationalism was more generally apparent in the 2010s than had been predicted.

Amis also caught Fleming's mood in Bond's attitude to politicians, with Sir Ranald Rideout, the minister responsible for the Secret Service, arrogant and stupid, adopting "an air of superiority in the presence of men worth twenty of him." He wears a "frilled azure evening shirt," a foppish and foolish garb, something both Fleming and Bond could have been expected to despise. Moreover, Rideout hates smokers, a trait Amis, a keen smoker, describes as psychopathic and associates with Hitler. This portrayal reflected a hostility toward politicians as complacent and duplicitous that was commonplace in adventure stories.

This hostility was accentuated for Amis by his dislike of the Labour government under Harold Wilson that was in power from 1964 to 1970 (and again from 1974 to 1976). This was a government very much not associated with the values of the past. In addition, MI5 kept a file on Wilson, whom they suspected of pro-Soviet leanings. There were persistent rumors, probably untrue, that he had been earlier recruited by the Soviets, notably when he had visited Moscow as President of the Board of Trade. However, as was suspected, some of his friends may have been Soviet agents in some respect or other. Bond, in contrast, is not a player in the cold corridors of governmental duplicity. His ironies are warmer, his deceits aimed at recognizable enemies. This is all part of his virility.

Kingsley Amis died in 1995, but in 1991, in advance of a new edition of *Colonel Sun*, he wrote an introduction that reflected on the task and on what he saw as key elements:

> the matter of setting, of *where*, so important in all Bond adventures. . . . I already knew a good deal about the question *why*—why Bond must go to Greece. . . . It took me two trips. . . . The first trip was to pick up ideas, the second to get the details right, essential in any Bond novel. It was no trouble at all to find the best olives, the best shellfish, the best local wine.

Amis also compared his writing with the way the Bond character had been transformed for the screen:

> Amis-style Bond found himself attacking the enemy with hand-grenades or a hunting knife, bolting sausages and fruit before the night assault, going in for the kill on his own two feet. No hovercraft, no helicopters, no rockets, and no double portions of Beluga caviar served in candlelit restaurants by white-jacketed waiters. He finds no use for the picklock and baby transmitter and the rest of the gadgets supplied by Q Branch on his departure. His own strength, determination and ingenuity are enough.
>
> The contrast is less with the original Bond, the real Bond of the Fleming novels, than with the Bond of the films, that rakish nonentity who drops yobbo-style throwaways out of the corner of his mouth before or after escaping by personal jet-pack or submersible car fitted with missile-launchers or (any moment) reactor-powered iceberg . . . the adolescent fantasies of the cinematic "James Bond."

This criticism was less significant than the wariness of the accountants, who were faceless figures rather than the equivalent of Truman Lodge in *Licence to Kill* (1989). This wariness was to the fore in 1991.

Bond had next returned, on the page, after a considerable gap, in 1981, with *Licence Renewed* by John Gardner, an established thriller writer. During the war, again World War II, he had trained in the Fleet Air Arm before transferring to the Royal Marines. After the war, he stayed on for some time and became a RAF chaplain, but was then discharged with a drink problem. As part of his rehabilitation, Gardner was advised to write it all down; hence his first book, *Spin the Bottle*. In *Licence Renewed*, the country had certainly lost direction, affected by political and economic lethargy and a short-term attitude to problems. Q branch was under severe financial restraint, and the 00 section had been abolished. A sense of passing values was provided by Bond's visit to the horse races at Royal Ascot. He was inspired by the sight of tradition as the royal family came down the course in their open carriages, but it was "a ceremony from another age." The ceremony, shown in *A View to a Kill* (1985), is in fact still followed in the late 2010s.

Six years later, in Gardner's *No Deals, Mr Bond* (1987), the sense of Britain on the slide was repeated. Murders were becoming more common, the elegant club Blades now needed money from foreign gamblers, a character claimed that the decadent British would fall because of self-indulgence and laxity, and Bond offered an ironic paean to Britain: "the click of willow against a villain's head, the roar of the riot, the scent of new-mown grass snakes." There had been large-scale riots in 1981 and 1985, and Gardner was clearly not sure that Mrs. Thatcher had revived Britain. Foreign money was certainly more present due to the "Big Bang" liberalization in the City of London in 1986, a measure that opened it to globalization.

The call of revolutionary virtue, however, is no answer. Indeed, repeatedly in the later novels, it is false virtues that are on offer, both flawed in themselves and exploited by villains—a theme echoed in some of the films, notably *Licence to Kill* (1989). In Gardner's novel *Scorpius* (1988), a freelance villain, Vladimir Scorpius, posing as Father Valentine, uses drugs and hypnotized religious followers in his English-based Society of Meek Ones, to try to assassinate major political figures. This novel drew on concern about religious cults.

In *Win, Lose or Die* (1989), BAST, the Brotherhood of Anarchy and Secret Terror, led by the avaricious Robert Besavitsky (a creation that is far less impressive than SPECTRE, while Besavitsky is no match for Blofeld), sought to benefit from the disaffected of the world, while also to trick his own deluded followers. The beautiful Clover Pennington explains to Bond, "Our kind of anarchy is positive. We want a fair and open society throughout the globe." Bond replies: "You're just like all those pipe dreamers, Clover. There'll never be a fair, free and open society in the world. You see, people get in the way. Ideals are for idealists, and all idealists fall from grace. No ideal works, simply because human beings cannot cope with it. . . . Power tends to corrupt; and absolute power corrupts absolutely."

The arrogant and deluded violence of the anarchists is a misled quest for virtue, but in Gardner's dyspeptic hands, Bond also repeatedly strikes the wrong note. In this novel, he goes for a stroll in the town of Woodstock, noting with disdain the aromas of cheap "pub grub. . . . He would, if pushed, like to see the countless young people crowding those very bars banished to some kind of National Service—preferably in the armed forces. That, he considered, would take violence off the streets of country towns, and make men out of the louts who littered pavements and got drunk at the sniff of a barmaid's apron." In practice, military commanders did not want the commitments, constraints, and costs of conscription, which had ended in Britain in the early 1960s.

"The thought of age and decay, of lost glory and of the current world tensions" that Bond experienced was part of a persona disenchanted with his society and hostile to change. The settings of the novels had to be exotic, in part because the readers and genre anticipated it, but also because the escapism was not only that of plot—resilience and success against the odds—but, crucially, also that of setting. In the Gardner novels, however, a characteristic of the Fleming approach, in this case disenchantment with the ordinary world, became overt and ugly. In part, this was because attitudes that were widely accepted when used by Fleming in the 1950s seemed misplaced in a different world. In part, this was also a matter of heavy-handedness; Fleming rarely had to state these attitudes and the related criticism of others. This heavy-handedness extended to the serious failure on Gardner's part to emulate the irony, style, and pace that had been so important in the Fleming novels. Gardner lacked Fleming's flair and his sense of irony. There was a glibness to Gardner's approach, as if he did not take the character seriously, and this gave his novels a very forced feel. Gardner's emphasis on race as a vital indicator of probity, as in the name and character of the villain, Besavitsky, was, by the 1980s, particularly misplaced. This was an aggressive twist to the earlier theme of deracination. Ultimately, *Win, Lose or Die*, like so many Bond plots, and indeed many of the Agatha Christie stories, was about maladjustment, specifically a failure to accept station.

The sense of society in Gardner's stories as under threat from challenges within was in part a response to the so-called death of history, more particularly the demise of the Soviet Union. This demise was resisted in Gardner's *The Man from Barbarossa* (1991), in which General Yevgeny Yuskovich, on behalf of "The Scales of Justice," has the modest aims of overthrowing the Russian government, reinstating Communism, helping Saddam Hussein, and destroying the United States with a nuclear strike. The 1990s very much represented an "in-between period": after the Cold War and before the "clash of civilizations." This was seen in the plots, notably *SeaFire* (1994), in which the villain, Sir Max Tarn, sought to re-create a Nazi regime with him as the new Führer, followed by *COLD* (1996), which in America appeared as *Cold Fall*. *COLD* involved the thwarting of General Brutus Clay's attempt to stage a Fascist coup in the United States on behalf of the Children of the Last Days (COLD).

Based on the screenplay of the film, Gardner also wrote the novel *GoldenEye* (1995); the differences are instructive. The scene near the beginning of the film in which Bond races a Ferrari on the Grand Corniche near Monte Carlo (a scene of excitement and a degree of humor, empty of concern), is preceded, in contrast, in the novel, by an angst-ridden passage revealing a nostalgia for the past and a concern, if not detestation, of the present:

> The south of France, Bond often reflected, was not what it used to be. The coastline . . . was packed to capacity during the season. The once leisurely Promenade des Anglais in Nice was even more leisurely, but today it was because of the steady slow-moving stream of traffic. . . . Bond detested the crowds, the traffic and the obvious growth of pollution, not only in the air, but also in the sea itself. There was trouble in what used to be paradise.

This approach was also seen in the description of Switzerland in Gardner's last Bond novel, *COLD*, as "a country displaying the less pleasant aspects of the drug subculture. . . . A few years ago, graffiti would have been unthinkable. Now it was the norm, as were the ragged unwashed teenagers who would never have been seen a decade before. In modern Switzerland the order and cleanliness were now only skin deep." This is very different to the Switzerland of the films *Goldfinger* (1964) and *On Her Majesty's Secret Service* (1969).

Gardner, who had lived in Charlottesville, Virginia, for many years, did not die until 2007; but he had already been replaced. His successor from 1996, Raymond Benson, was an American board member of the Ian Fleming Foundation, based in the United States. He had written *The James Bond Bedside Companion* (1984), and sought to present Fleming's Bond free from political correctness and with all vices intact. Benson's tone was less harsh than Gardner's; it is more pleasant to read his novels. They were also more optimistic than those of Fleming, at least in the sense that Bond does not collapse as a character. Written in 1996, Benson's first adventure, "Blast from the Past," was a short story published in *Playboy* in January 1997. Set in London and New York, this was a sequel to the Blofeld stories, in which Irma Bunt sought revenge for the close of *You Only Live Twice*: both for her injuries and for Blofeld's death. The plot included some psychological depth, notably Bond's relationship with his son and the death of the latter. The return and death of Bunt, and her torture of Bond, provide the dynamic of the story.

As with Gardner, there was from Benson a mixture of books based on screenplays, and also freestanding adventures, such as *Zero Minus Ten* (1997). This was an attack on the corruption and squalor of China but also a defense of Chinese people against the racism of the villain, who seeks the nuclear devastation of Hong Kong to provoke war between Britain and China. In his *Tomorrow Never Dies* (1997), Benson claimed that Elliot Carver, the villain, directed his anger against Britain because of his origins as the illegitimate son of a perverted British media lord. The weight of origins, notably illegitimacy, was a theme of many "Golden Age" writers, notably Agatha Christie. The books that are film scripts written up, or that read as if they were, are weakened, however, by lacking independence and even integrity.

Benson, in turn, has been succeeded by a number of more major writers, each writing on a one-off basis. Some have been more successful than others. Sebastian Faulks's *Devil May Care* (2008) has problems. Faulks made a reasonable approximation of Fleming's literary style. Fleming of course wrote in his time, while Faulks did so in a "retro" style. That said, the decision to set it in period was reasonable. The Gardner and Benson books never had the right "feel": partly the style, but also partly the setting. However, Faulks's villain, Gorner, was weak, despite the grotesque deformity he is given, and some of Gardner's villains were better (such as in *Brokenclaw*). In a characteristic Fleming feature, Gorner moved from the Nazis to the Soviets. The conspiracy in *Devil May Care* appeared more inspired by the films, especially the film of *Live and Let Die* with its drugs plot, than the novels, and the second half of the novel, following Bond's capture, seemed to be Bond-by-numbers. This half was also anticlimactic:

the long trek across Russia (vast distances covered rather too quickly and too easily) is a letdown after the scene on the aircraft. While it lasted, *Devil May Care* was enjoyable, but few readers were or are in a hurry to read it again, whereas many can reread Fleming every few years and still enjoy the prose. *Devil May Care* started off as something close to a Fleming Bond, but, by the end, had turned into a Gardner Bond.

In contrast, William Boyd's *Solo* (2013) was well written, indeed rather better written than Fleming. Drawing on his African expertise, Boyd, a highly experienced novelist, had the clever idea of putting Bond into the (disguised) Biafran War of 1967–1970 at the right time during 007's career. This approach suggests that, as a character in fiction, Bond still enjoys considerable traction. This has been taken further with the presentation of Bond in a series of other novels, most notably for children.

Rereading Fleming, his range and immediacy strike hard. He is an economic writer who is an effective storyteller. In addition, Bond is an interesting and complex protagonist—one who is far more on show than either Holmes or Poirot. Fleming can deftly create suspense, as in *Moonraker*, a suspense that matched the energy of the films. At the same time, there is a literary reflection not seen in the films. For example, take Bond's reflection on the tale of infidelity and personal drama he hears in Nassau in "Quantum of Solace":

> Bond laughed. Suddenly the violent dramatics of his own life seemed very hollow. The affair of the Castro rebels and the burned out yachts was the stuff of an adventure-strip in a cheap newspaper. He had sat next to a dull woman at a dull dinner party and a chance remark had opened for him the book of real violence—the Comédie Humaine where human passions are raw and real, where Fate plays a more authentic game than any Secret Service conspiracy devised by Governments.

Maybe so for Fleming, but not for his readers and, even more, viewers-to-be.

4

BOND HITS THE SCREEN

Fleming's Bond is repeatedly under destructive psychological pressure, his obituary indeed appearing at the end of *You Only Live Twice* (1964). This would, on the pattern of Sherlock Holmes and his supposed fall into the Reichenbach Falls, have offered an opportunity to write him out of fictional life, as also earlier in the close of *From Russia, With Love*, when Bond takes a blow in his shins from a knife in Rosa Klebb's shoe. Instead, Bond was brought back again, only for it to be revealed in the last full-length novel, *The Man with the Golden Gun* (1965), that he had been brainwashed by the Soviets. This explains Bond's attempt to kill M at the start of the story. The character has only limited traction by 1964, and Fleming, indeed, appeared fed up. By then, however, Bond had been both transferred to the cinema and totally reinvented on screen—and successfully so. America plays the crucial role. Bond is not the tested, even at times broken, figure who appears in the novels. Instead, he is an untroubled man of action.

And one who delivers results. In particular, in the films, Bond dramatically, and frequently, saved America. After all, as the seconds ticked away toward the close of the films, he stopped Dr. No from "toppling" a crucial American missile test (1962); prevented

Goldfinger from making the Fort Knox gold reserves radioactive (1964); thwarted Largo's attempt to blow up Miami (*Thunderball*, 1965), and Blofeld's to destroy Washington (the villain rejects Kansas—"the world might not notice," *Diamonds Are Forever*, 1971), as well as Zorin's plan for the devastation of Silicon Valley (*A View to a Kill*, 1985). Bond also defeats other megalomaniacs. Some of these, such as Stromberg in *The Spy Who Loved Me* (1977) and Drax in *Moonraker* (1979), would have destroyed America as part of a total global cataclysm.

Bond may have appeared to save America, but, in fact, it was America that saved Bond, just as America had helped save Britain and Western values, both in World War II and in the Cold War. Bond was originally a quintessentially British figure, but he was translated for the film role. Indeed, the modern world knows Bond through the films, not the novels. The intentions of Fleming are glimpsed at second hand, and even then only fitfully so after the third film, *Goldfinger*, which appeared in 1964, the year of his early death. His character, Bond, and the titles of his stories, but not the plots or the context, are what is left.

Ironically, the first portrayal of Bond on screen was as an American, "Jimmy Bond," ably played as a heavy-smoking hard man, by Barry Nelson. This was in a 1954 black-and-white hour-long CBS live studio–shot television version of *Casino Royale* entitled *Too Hot to Handle*, in the *Climax Mystery Theater* series, broadcast on October 21. In contrast to the novel, it was the British agent, now called Clarence Leiter, who assisted Bond, so that the Anglo-American relationship of the book was reversed for American consumption. This approach matched America's perception of the Anglo-American relationship in World War II and thereafter. Peter Lorre, who played the villain Le Chiffre, was shot dead at the close of the television version (as in the story), but, unaware that the cameras were still rolling, he got up and walked off. "Jimmy Bond" was also the name of a character in the 2001 American television series *The Lone Gunmen*, a largely comic series.

With the exception of this television version of *Casino Royale*, Fleming's hopes of Bond being presented on the screen, and of the author gaining much money and fame accordingly, had for long been unsuccessful. Financial backing, or rather the absence of it, was a key element. This lack of success reflected the inherent cost of the Bond plots, but also the studios' perception that American viewers would not necessarily be interested in a British secret agent. It long proved impossible to obtain the necessary financial backing, and Fleming encountered a series of problems in winning support. These included, in Britain, Alexander Korda's failure to follow through on a 1953 approach to Fleming about taking Bond to the screen. In his copy of *Moonraker*, Fleming noted "It is based on a film script I have had in my mind for many many years." When *Casino Royale* was released as a book in the United States in March 1954, it had mixed reviews, notably in the *New York Times*, and sold only 4,000 copies in its first year, its year in hardback only.

Fleming's quest for American support was more than just a matter of money. It also reflected his fascination, and that of many postwar Britons, with the United States as a land of opulence. Thus, in *Goldfinger*, Bond is collected in Miami in a "gleaming Chrysler Imperial. . . . The soft upholstery. The interior of the car was deliciously cool . . . carried along on the gracious stream of speed and comfort and rich small-talk." He goes on to an excellent meal, and to an opulent hotel the details of which are lovingly presented. There was also something sympathetic to America about a British agent who was revealed by Fleming as not drinking tea, thinking it mud, and, instead, preferring coffee.

In 1961, Harry Saltzman, a Canadian-born film producer, bought a six-month option on the Bond stories but was unable to obtain backing to produce them until he teamed up with Albert

"Cubby" Broccoli, an American producer, eventually setting up Danjaq to hold the copyrights and Eon Productions to produce the films. Broccoli helped Saltzman finance the deal, which acquired the film rights to all the novels that Fleming owned, which excluded, as it turned out, *Casino Royale*, to which the permanent screen rights had been sold for $6,000 in 1955, and *Thunderball*, the character Blofeld, and SPECTRE. Broccoli and Saltzman also acquired the film rights to the character of Bond, which meant that they could continue the series once the novels had all been filmed. At that stage, there were only six novels and a collection of short stories. Fleming was to receive £100,000 for each title, plus 2.5 percent of the net profits from each film, and a title had to be optioned every eighteen months. Broccoli and Saltzman persuaded United Artists to provide the money needed for the production, which was their key role: Fleming needed intermediaries. Moreover, Broccoli and Saltzman established the tone of the series.

Thunderball was to be the first film, but bitter legal disputes over copyright that went to court led to the substitution of *Dr. No*. The dispute over *Thunderball* with Kevin McClory was agreed out of court in November 1963, with McClory, who had a good case, to receive the screen rights. Excluding the parody *Casino Royale* (1967) and *Never Say Never Again* (1983), a remake of *Thunderball*, the films have all been the work of Eon Productions. Broccoli eventually bought Saltzman out, and his family has retained control since. From *The Spy Who Loved Me* (1977), Broccoli was sole producer of the Eon films. In 2013, McClory's estate sold the rights to MGM, which enabled Eon to use SPECTRE in the next film.

Dr. No itself as a novel had been Fleming's reworking of a TV pilot, *James Gunn—Secret Agent*, that he had written in 1956 for a planned American television series that was never made, part of a series of disappointments. Setting it in Jamaica, still then a Brit-

ish colony, ensured that the film would receive British financial
support. The film began with two views of empire—views not
intended to suggest that empire was on the eve of dissolution.
The Kingston Club, the center of white, male society in Jamaica,
is followed by imperial Westminster, in the shape of a night shot
of Big Ben and the Thames, as a prelude to the scene in the
society casino *Le Cercle*.

In contrast to the slow and scarcely credible start of the novel,
with its implausible explanation of MI6 involvement, the film rapidly sets out massive interference with the American Cape Canaveral rocket tests as the key political element. In the first treatment
by the screenwriters, the locks on the Panama Canal, then
American-run, are Dr. No's target, which again reflects the focus
on American hemispheric and geopolitical interests. The intention of Dr. No's plot was to cause American-Soviet conflict in the
Caribbean, with a Chinese criminal society benefiting. A second
version of the film treatment had the Chinese government benefiting. Finally, SPECTRE was pushed to the fore and references
to a Cuban agent were dropped.

Whereas in the novel Felix Leiter plays no role, America is to
the fore in the film, as is the competition with the Chinese in the
person of Dr. No and his associates: Chinese men in uniform
appear in the doctor's entourage. An initial draft of the screenplay
had suggested a spider monkey or chimpanzee sitting on the
shoulder of the villain, a device that was not followed. This proved
a step into the bizarre that was too far for Bond, but apes as the
villains, finally discovered controlling a mysterious secret world
where a British secret agent, played by Patrick McGoohan, was
imprisoned, were subsequently used for the British television series *The Prisoner*.

The theme of Oriental menace both recycled earlier treatments, notably the Fu Manchu stories, and more immediate contemporary concerns that, in America, were focused on China and

Southeast Asia, first Laos and then Vietnam. Britain was involved in a limited conflict with Indonesia in 1962–1966, but the Orient played a much smaller role in British than in American anxieties. The Chinese also played sinister roles in the films of *Goldfinger* (1964) and *You Only Live Twice* (1967), although not in the books, while, in *Thunderball* (1965), SPECTRE distributes Chinese drugs in the United States. The setting in the Caribbean also captured contemporary interest in Cuba: 1961 saw the Bay of Pigs. The British premiere of *Dr. No* was on October 5, 1962, shortly before the Cuban missile crisis nearly took the world to war, but the film was not launched in the United States until May 1963. The Communist power in that case was the Soviet Union, not China. The year 1962, however, also saw a successful Chinese attack on Indian forces in the Himalayas—an attack that contributed to a sense of threat and that underlined the limited palette of options available to the West.

The Chinese threat had not been a particular theme of the novels, although in the novel *Goldfinger*, when Bond returns to London from Mexico, he authorizes the dispatch of limpet mines to Hong Kong, still then a British colony, "to put paid to those Communist spy junks that were using Macao to intercept British freighters and search them for refugees from China." Bond reflected:

> He'd never liked being up against the Chinese. There were too many of them. Station H might be stirring up a hornets' nest, but M had decided it was time to show the opposition that the service in Hongkong [*sic*] hadn't quite gone out of business.

In a major contrast to the novels, *Dr. No* introduces SPECTRE into the films from the start; Dr. No is a member who wishes to look Bond over to see whether he can be recruited. Rather than focusing on the Cold War, Dr. No, like SPECTRE, is free of alignments, and, indeed, by Dr. No's view of universal

WITH AN INTRODUCTION
BY LOUISE WELSH

007 IAN
FLEMING

A JAMES BOND NOVEL

LIVE
AND LET
DIE

Live and Let Die, originally published in 1954.

Dr. No, 1962. The poster for the first James Bond film very much put the emphasis on the women. The villain was overshadowed by their lineup.

From Russia, With Love, 1963. Again, the women took center stage in the poster. The dramatic fight on the train was not hinted at. Bond looked saturnine.

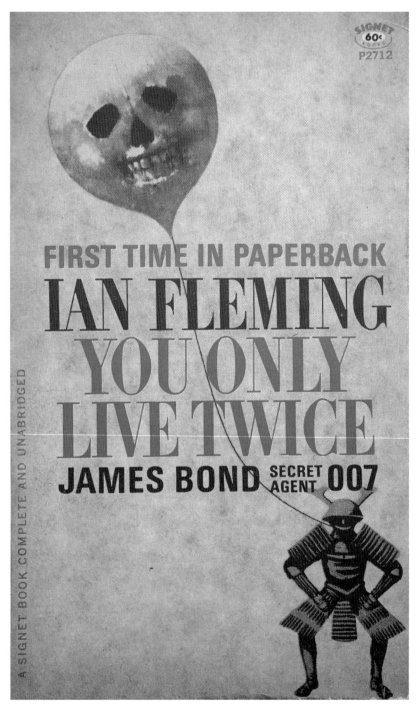

SIGNET
60¢
P2712

FIRST TIME IN PAPERBACK

IAN FLEMING
YOU ONLY
LIVE TWICE
JAMES BOND SECRET AGENT 007

A SIGNET BOOK COMPLETE AND UNABRIDGED

You Only Live Twice, originally published in 1964.

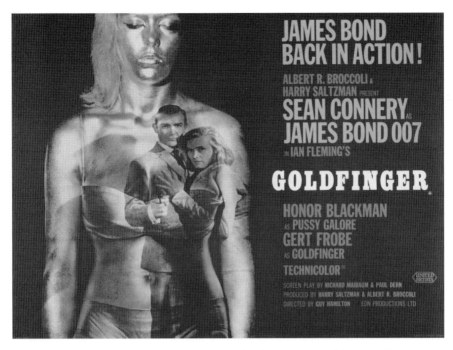

Goldfinger, 1964. Gold predominated in the poster, although in the film the dead, gold-covered Jill Masterson was depicted as naked.

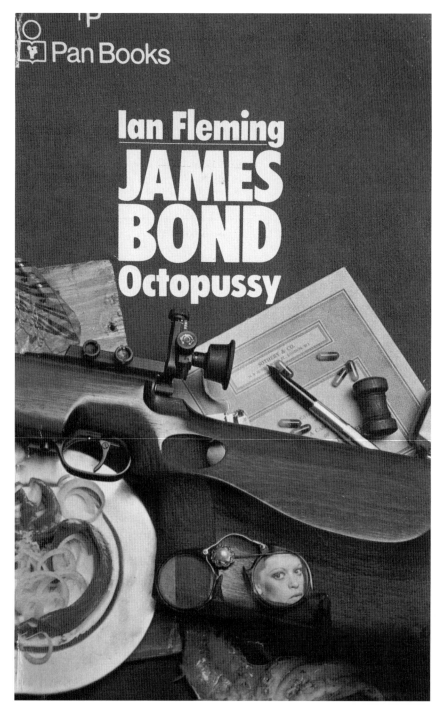

Octopussy, originally published in 1966.

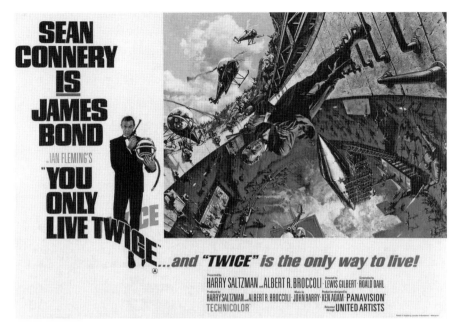

You Only Live Twice, 1967. The poster captured the dramatic battle at the close of the film and the set created for it.

Colonel Sun, originally published in 1968.

On Her Majesty's Secret Service, 1969. Ski chases and a helicopter assault both played a role in the film. The poster did not push sex to the fore.

Diamonds Are Forever, 1971. Bond between two competing women was a theme on the cover of the dramatic, exploding poster.

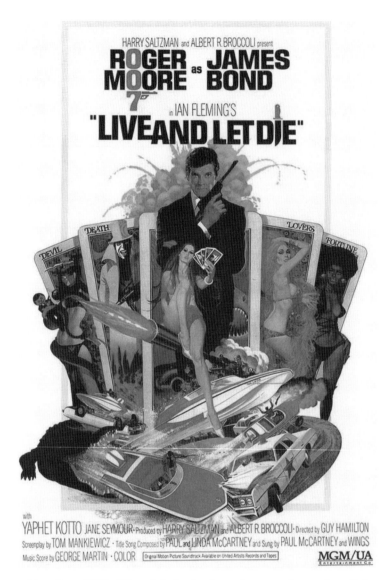

Live and Let Die, 1973. **The tightly designed poster brought all the themes of the film together in an effective montage of drama, violence, and menace.**

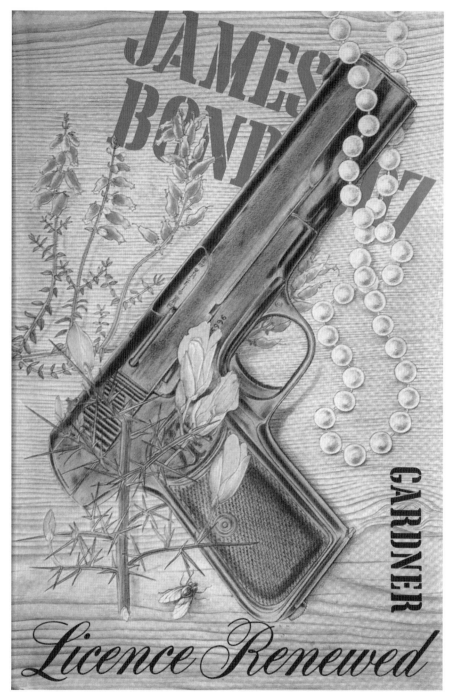

Licence Renewed, originally published in 1981.

The Living Daylights, 1987. The crowded poster captured the some-what confused plot, which struggled to comprehend a range of story-lines.

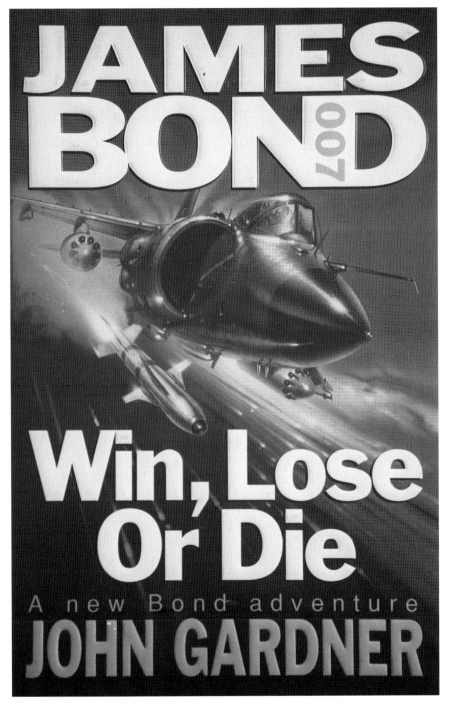

Win, Lose or Die, originally published in 1987.

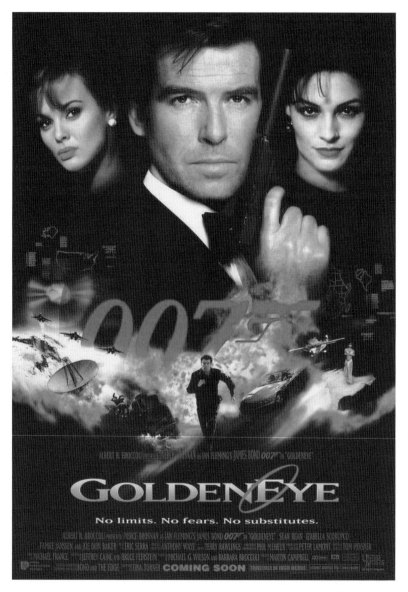

GoldenEye, 1995. A new Bond, the first for the post–Cold War, although it was the new **M** that was a more abrupt change.

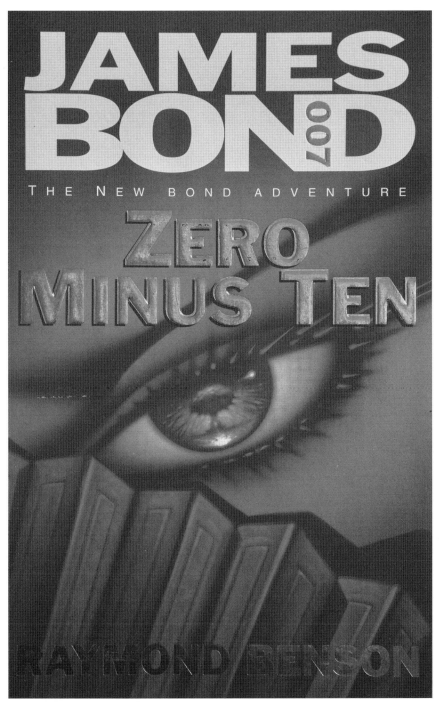

Zero Minus Ten, originally published in 1997.

Skyfall, 2012. Daniel Craig, a Bond who could convey menace, provided an effective prop to take an old franchise forward.

predation—"East, West . . . points of the compass,"—ironically frequently emphasizes East-West shared interests. The broader pattern of the films was set by *Dr. No*: Bond's mission became a quest to stop the villain, a theme that focused on confrontations between the captive Bond and his megalomaniacal adversary. To the latter, Bond is an irritant, a distraction from the doom of a decadent civilization, but, in fact, Bond becomes the nemesis of the villain who says he never fails. Bond's boldness and the villain's hubris are instrumental in the outcome, and repeatedly so.

The film offered gadgets, but certainly not at the rate of later films. The cars are traditional, notably in the chases on Jamaica, and there is no interest in aircraft. The major surprise is a dragon that turns out to be a flame-throwing vehicle in disguise, and that, in practice, is rather low-tech and not particularly gripping. Nor were the fights on the level of later films. On the other hand, the dialogue was good on the parts of Bond and the villain. Dr. No calls Bond "a stupid policeman whose luck has run out," but a brutal side is shown in Bond's killing of Professor Dent, a Dr. No agent, and in his harsh treatment of women. Connery's characterization of Bond was the major legacy of the film, but a lot else was offered, including the theme music, the exotic setting, what became the standard scene with M, the girls, the attempts to kill Bond, and the mysterious and sinister villain who is based in a large and dramatic structure.

The film provided a very different plot, pace, and timescale from those of the novel in that the threat to American rockets is revealed in M's meeting with Bond, whereas in the novel it comes near the close as part of the solution of a puzzle. Moreover, in the film, the plot lasts four days, not the six weeks of the novel. This provides immediacy, drama, and pace. The murder of Dent— "That's a Smith and Wesson . . . and you've had your six [bullets]," so that Bond can shoot him with impunity, gave Bond a definite edge. A would-be murderer is shot dead when he is no longer a threat. This scene invited the outrage of some critics, but then they were never going to applaud it. The presentation of Leiter began that of a series of cameos of CIA operatives—a series that emphasized the appearance in the films of the Anglo-American "Special Relationship."

Costing $950,000, *Dr. No* made vast profits, both for the film-makers, grossing $2 million in North America and $4 million abroad, and for the publishers, leading to the sale of 1.5 million copies of the book within seven months of the appearance of the film. Popularity and profit subsequently increased. As a result of the success of *Dr. No*, United Artists raised the budget allowed per film from $1 million to $2 million, which very much put the intended outcome in a different league of film-making. Bond clearly was not going to be a "B movie" hero. The investment worked. In Britain, 200,000 viewers saw *From Russia, With Love* (1963) in the first week of its release, while, in France, a million viewers saw it within a month in 1964, the centerpiece of a major triumph for the film in Western Europe. Other major markets included Italy and West Germany.

The screen persona of Bond was set. He was not to have the introspection of Fleming's creation, and that was an important aspect of the Americanization of Bond. Indeed, although deriving money and fame from the films, Fleming was unhappy with them. He had seen *Dr. No* being made in Jamaica, but responded with hostility to the preview he attended in London—"Dreadful. Simply dreadful." Crucially, however, this was not his public view. In an interview in October 1962 with *Time*, an American publication, Fleming predicted that readers of his *Dr. No* would find the film a disappointment, but that those who had not read the book would "find it a wonderful movie." This was well-judged praise; most filmgoers, particularly in the United States, had not read the novels.

As in the novels, Bond's mission was necessary as well as legitimate, decided by a secret service that was unimpeachable. This was a moral absolute that very much differentiated Bond from the novels and film versions of Len Deighton's *The Ipcress File* and John Le Carré's *The Spy Who Came in from the Cold*, both of which reached the cinema in 1965. These films were also far grittier than the Bond films. Instead, the Bond films matched the agent's omnicompetence, presence, and bravery to a clear moral purpose. Thus, the Bond films took the Westerns of the period and applied them to the current world. Bond stands for integrity in every sense, whereas his deceitful opponents practice disguise. This integrity is that of the organization, but also that of the individual. The latter brings together the adventure story with the emphasis on the capacity of individuals, a capacity very much linked to Bond's appeal to women and his ability to win their backing. This is very different to the cruel and vicious modus operandi of his megalomaniacal opponents.

The Bond portrayal suggests that the traditions of the British imperial elite have something to offer the Americans: a style that also has substance. Sean Connery was well placed to manage this transition, and better so than Broccoli's original choices, Cary Grant and David Niven. Fleming had wanted Niven, a stylish public-school gent, who was more Fleming's vintage, to play Bond; but Broccoli sought a tougher, mid-Atlantic image, able to appeal to American filmgoers as a man of action without putting them off with jarring British mannerisms. Roger Moore appeared somewhat effete and was under contract for *The Saint* series, while Patrick McGoohan, who later starred in *The Prisoner*, thought the role unacceptable on moral grounds. Bond had to be self-contained, not self-satisfied, and thus, with Connery, a star was born. While able to present himself as a traditional gentleman, as in the dinner-jacketed casino scene in *Dr. No*, this son of an Edinburgh delivery driver, himself a former milkman, was also a modernizing figure. This was apparent both in the sophisticated ironic comedy that Connery offered in his repartee, on the pattern of Cary Grant, and in his engagement with new technology, speed, and an easy style.

Described by *Film Daily* as "a winning mixture of urbanity and masculinity," Connery provided Broccoli with what he wanted, an adventure hero for a mass audience. Able to radiate clarity of purpose and, crucially, a physical menace in his body language, and to move with danger as if a big cat with deadly claws and silent purpose, Bond appeared less establishment, certainly less polished, than the aloof Julius No. He is the active figure who has to protect the colonial ease of Jamaica from a threatening, dangerous, and almost unknowable outsider.

The role was in part defined by Connery and by the director, Terence Young. There was a lot of improvisation on the set: for example, Bond's line "I think they were on their way to a funeral," after the pursuing car carrying his would-be assassins fatally plunged into a gorge in Jamaica. Young allowed and encouraged this improvisation. Another actor would probably have chosen other improvisations, and thus created a different persona and film.

Broccoli and Richard Maibaum, who was chief screenwriter for thirteen Bond films, were Americans, Saltzman Canadian, and George Lazenby Australian, but the creative team was largely British. This was true of the directors, of whom the first two were Terence Young and Guy Hamilton. The first non-British director was Martin Campbell, who directed *GoldenEye* (1995). Ken Adam, who created the sets, was born in Germany, but his family fled to Britain in 1934, and during World War II he flew a Hawker Typhoon tank-buster. The main composer, John Barry, who created the "James Bond Sound" and wrote most of the good title songs, was British, as was Monty Norman, who wrote the James Bond theme. The title songs were to be an important feature of the Bond films. Sung slowly and with distinct and distinctive lyrics, they were important to the construction of particular images and moods for individual films.

The very introduction of Bond in *Dr. No* provides an impression of power. The "Bond . . . James Bond" amid the cigarette smoke, the killer in the dinner jacket, is not intended as a spy who gives a few jolly slaps and takes part in a stylized fight. He has power, but also style. The director, Young, moved Connery to be more Fleming's Bond than the son of Edinburgh poverty. Young changed his image, not least by getting him clothes he thought appropriate, and introduced Connery to golf, such that he did not need a double for the golf in *Goldfinger*, unlike Gert Fröbe, who played Goldfinger. Fleming had even less appropriately suggested his friend and neighbor in Jamaica, Noel Coward, to play the villainous Julius No.

The theme of Bond as a brutal, but stylish, protector was taken forward in *From Russia, With Love* (1963), with SPECTRE under Blofeld, his ideas man and expert chess player Kronsteen, and his agents, Rosa Klebb and Donald "Red" Grant, played by Lotte Lenya and Robert Shaw, seeking to exploit the established struggle between Britain and the Soviet Union. This is presented as a rivalry that is relatively calm and well ordered, but it is one that SPECTRE aims to exacerbate in order to provide it with opportunities and get its plot to work. Blofeld explains this in terms of the Siamese fighting fish he demonstrates: SPECTRE waits to see which one would win and would then fight the exhausted victor.

Unusually, this was a film without America or the Americans (although Bond flies Pan Am to Istanbul), except that it benefited from Kennedy choosing the novel for a *Life* article on March 17, 1961, about his reading habits. It was given as one of his ten favorites; the article noted Kennedy's "weakness for detective stories, especially those of British author Ian Fleming." The film indeed was the last Kennedy saw. He watched it the night before he left for Texas in November 1963. Britain plays a crucial role but this is a result of a choice by the villain. This was explained as revenge for Dr. No, who was a SPECTRE operative: Blofeld calls for a particularly unpleasant and humiliating death for Bond. Another continuation from *Dr. No* is that Bond at the outset of the new film is kissing in a punt with Sylvia French, the woman he has had sex with after meeting at the casino at the outset of *Dr. No*. She was then dropped from the Bond films.

The settings were excellent, notably the varied offerings of Istanbul above and below ground, the Orient Express, the Yugoslav countryside, and Venice. This location shooting reflected the increased budget. There was an air of suspense from the outset, when, in a teaser sequence, Bond is stalked by Grant through a garden before being garroted. A rubber mask on Bond's face then reveals him to be really a SPECTRE agent in a life-training exercise. Britain is also still able to play a crucial role, and in a region where its power had been significant for over a century. The Balkans was an established beat for British adventure stories, notably those of Fleming's contemporary Eric Ambler, which Fleming liked.

The challenge was not only political. With his clipped accent, Grant was a figure of menace. Later impersonating a British agent he has murdered at a train stop for the Orient Express, he was also a challenge to social positioning, ordering the wrong wine—chianti—with his fish, which Bond criticizes accordingly.

There were a number of dramatic fights in the film, notably the Bulgarian attack on the gypsy camp outside Istanbul, the lengthy fight between Grant and Bond on the train, which was used in the trailer, and the lethal and clever Bond subsequently taking out the helicopter and, later, boats hunting him across Yugoslavia. The gadgets were more impressive than in *Dr. No*, but less so than they were to be in *Goldfinger*. Aside from Klebb's shoe with the poisoned knife, and the Russian Lektor decoder, which is based on Fleming's knowledge of the Enigma machine, Bond has a pager and car phone, and later Q branch provides him with a leather case that includes an exploding cartridge of tear gas in a tin of talcum powder, a folding sniper's rifle with infrared sights, gold sovereigns, ammunition, and a throwing knife. The weapons are necessary to the killing of Grant and, later, the destruction of the helicopter. Both prove crucial in Bond's survival.

Earlier, Bond is briefed for the first time by Desmond Llewellyn as Q, for Quartermaster, and the film saw the first pre-title action sequence and the first hit theme song. Other firsts included the first appearance of Blofeld and his white Persian cat. At the end, a closing caption promised another Bond film.

With profits assured and money available, *Goldfinger* (1964) followed rapidly. Connery again played Bond, now far more assured than in the earlier films, both because he was more experienced and because Terence Young did not direct the film. Connery also received much more money. The audience knew what to expect, which helped greatly. *Goldfinger* took Bond to the United States for the first time in the films, with an early scene in a Miami hotel. After lengthy passages in Britain and Switzerland, the rest of the film took place in Goldfinger's ranch in Kentucky and in Fort Knox, also in Kentucky. The film brought together style, setting, and technology under the care of a new director, Guy Hamilton, who had turned down *Dr. No*. The trailer described Bond as the "toughest, wiliest gentleman agent," adding "the hotter the danger the cooler he takes it." In the pre-credits adventure, Bond takes off his wet suit to reveal a white tuxedo, before putting a flower in his buttonhole. The plot showed Britain in difficulties, with Goldfinger, dressing in tweed like a British gentleman, owning the traditional-style gold club and therefore able to have his bowler-hatted servant Oddjob decapitate a statue with his flying hat.

However, America itself is vulnerable. The threat to the gold reserves in Fort Knox was in part a reference to the vulnerability of America's international position and to the precariousness of the gold-based Bretton Woods agreement on fixed exchange rates for currencies. The scheme would have represented a clear and present danger to the very fabric of the postwar American-dominated world economy, and might have resonated as such among more globally minded American viewers at the time of its debut.

Goldfinger uses the Mob to get his attack force assembled and armed in America, but then readily disposes of the Mob leaders. The military is his next target. Goldfinger is able to get an atom bomb into Fort Knox and to spray Delta Nine invisible nerve gas over the nearby American army base. This was a far more threatening plot than *From Russia, With Love*. Goldfinger's deadliness is indicated by his dismissal of the likely 60,000 deaths that would result by saying that that was only two years' deaths on the road. Such a comparison remains possible. America's geopolitical concerns are noted with Goldfinger supported by China and on his way to Cuba at the end.

Aside from glamorous settings and women, *Goldfinger* had technology. The villain deployed an industrial laser beam, the first display of a laser on film, and a substitute to the revolving buzz-saw of the novel. Bond had a nimble, fast Aston Martin DB-5 that included, among its armaments, machine guns, a smoke screen, a radar tracker, a capacity to drop oil on the road, bulletproof windshields, tire shredders in the hubcaps, and, most dramatically, an ejector seat. This actually worked, using compressed air and a dummy. Two million of the miniature version made by Corgi Toys were sold. I, indeed, had one and was very proud to own it.

Spectacle was provided by the sets of the production designer, Ken Adam, notably with the shining gold vault of Fort Knox and with Goldfinger's operations room in Kentucky. There was also a superb film score, a powerful theme song brilliantly sung by Shirley Bassey, and a dramatic, engaging, and witty pre-credits teaser that underlined Bond's style.

The film was a tremendous financial success. The top release in Britain, it was the fastest-grossing film yet made in the United States. For the first fourteen weeks, North American takings were $10,374,807. It recouped its $3.5 million budget in a fortnight, becoming the fastest-grossing film hitherto and earning a total of nearly $50 million worldwide. *Playboy* proclaimed Bond the hero of the age. Sales of the book benefited. The paperback had been first published in Britain in 1961 and was reprinted twice that year, with three reprintings in 1962, four in 1963, and seven in 1964. Sales of the other books also took off. First published in paperback in Britain in 1963, *Thunderball* was reprinted four times that year alone. Other Bond products also took off. *Time* noted on February 26, 1965, that a "Bond market" existed "From London to Los Angeles," producing Bond clothing, jewelry, pajamas, vodka, and golf clubs.

Goldfinger's success ensured bigger budgets for later films, which meant they could be longer and could contain more special effects. Both were seen in *Thunderball* (1965), which was overlong but contained what was a novel amount of filming of underwater action scenes. Initially, Kevin McClory, who held the screen rights, had proposed to make the film himself, with the plot focusing on the theft of a hydrogen bomb and the world being held for ransom. In the end, however, he approached Eon with the idea of a co-production. Eon accepted, ensuring that *Thunderball* was the next film and not, as originally intended, *On Her Majesty's Secret Service*. McClory was not to direct it as he had first wanted, and Terence Young was again appointed instead, with a $5.6 million budget and the use of the 1961 screenplay by Richard Maibaum.

The cast was cosmopolitan. The villain Emilio Largo, SPECTRE's No. 2, was ably played by Adolfo Celi, while Claudine

Auger made a good Domino, and Luciana Paluzzi played glamorous SPECTRE assassin Fiona Volpe well. The film also had a superb title song by Tom Jones. In the pre-credits adventure, set in France, the exposure of the cross-dressing Colonel Jacques Boitier, a SPECTRE agent, and his killing by Bond before the latter escapes by Bell Textron jet pack, was dramatic. The plot moved on to England, including assassination by Volpe on a rocket-firing motorbike. Then on to the Bahamas.

As in the novel, a British bomber and its atom bombs were stolen, a testimony to Britain's continued military power and an explanation of Bond's role. So also was reference in the film to aircraft refueling in the British base in Aden, whence, in practice, a Soviet-backed guerrilla campaign was to lead to a humiliating British withdrawal in 1967.

Having beaten off sharks in the Caribbean, Bond saves the situation, locating the bombs, but the key military elements in the close of the film were American: aircraft, frogmen parachuting in, and warships. Miami was the backdrop to the last showdown. The proximity of the Bahamas provided Britain with a regional presence, but the realities now of a film set in the Caribbean were those offered by American power and proximity. More significantly, the world premiere, on December 21, 1965, was in New York, London following eight days later. The commercial thrust had moved. Again the films were helping the sales of the novels, which had reached about sixty million by the time *Thunderball* was released.

The scenes were on a formidable scale, with over fifty divers in the final lengthy underwater battle. The US Navy provided underwater equipment and the "Skyhook" rescue system used at the end. The film won an Oscar for special visual effects. Skills were also necessary in filming the shark fight. Bond's exchanges with Volpe were brilliant, as was his escape from the shark pool. There was an edginess to the violence and to the sex: Bond finds

Volpe a rough sexual partner, and then she is very willing to have him killed. However, as with her earlier killing of Count Lippe, a SPECTRE agent who had failed, Volpe is killed by a SPECTRE assassin, although, in this case, accidentally, because a quick-moving Bond has thwarted the SPECTRE plan to have him shot. Incredibly successful, including in France, Italy, and Japan, the film's worldwide gross was $141.2 million. The success led to the rerelease of earlier Bond films.

This success was not to be matched by *Casino Royale* (1967). A Bond story outside Eon's scope, the film was financed by Columbia, which had failed in 1965 to purchase Eon. The film rights belonged to Charles Feldman who, in turn, had been unable to persuade Broccoli to cooperate in producing the picture. With $6 million of Columbia's money, Feldman faced a host of problems, including the death of Ben Hecht before he had finished the screenplay. A whole host of writers provided script. Initially, Feldman approached Connery, who was committed to Eon and asked for $1 million, which Feldman refused. Connery having turned him down, Feldman, who had done very well financially with the flippant *What's New Pussycat?* (1965), decided on a spoof, which led to a total rewriting, focused also on bringing in Peter Sellers for a different role. David Niven was brought in to star as a retired Bond. Other stars included Ursula Andress, the female lead in *Dr. No.* A torrent of rearrangements caused cascading delays, which were interspersed with rows and walk-offs, including of Sellers (who loathed Orson Welles, who played Le Chiffre) and of the directors. The film was reconceptualized as a series of sections, each with different directors, but even that brought no fixity. Continuity, plot, and credibility were lost, amid critical press reports about the production, which was increasingly delayed. Columbia had to pay up $12 million, while Feldman suffered a heart attack. Instead of being released for Christmas 1966, the film appeared in April 1967. The press coverage was eviscerating. The focus of the criticism was on the senselessness of the plot. Nevertheless, the fashion for Bond led the film to make a profit. Because of the delay until 1967, *Casino Royale* may have hit the takings of *You Only Live Twice*, which also appeared in 1967.

Casino Royale is noted for its number of Bonds: the agents are given the codename "James Bond, 007." The SMERSH flying saucer is a particular plot device, as is the Doctor Noah, the SMERSH head, who is really Bond's nephew, Jimmy Bond (a young Woody Allen), who, in a revenge of the shorts, wants to destroy all men over four foot six. The totally implausible gadgets included machine guns in bagpipes and bowler hat guns. Niven's Sir James Bond is given a series of put-down lines to direct at Connery's Bond:

> In my day spying was an alternative to war, and the spy was a member of a select and immaculate priesthood—vocationally devoted, sublimely disinterested. Hardly a description of that sexual acrobat who leaves a trail of beautiful dead women like blown roses behind him. That bounder to whom you gave my name and number. . . . Him and his wretched gadgets . . . joke shop spies.

The film had humor, a marvelous song in "The Look of Love," and some good performances. While being totally different, the film is not necessarily any more different to the novels than many of the later Bond films. However, the plot was very weak and extremely muddled, and its presentation confused and confusing.

You Only Live Twice, which had its world premiere in London on June 12, 1967, with the Queen in the audience, took Bond to Japan. This was both the setting of the novel of that name, and another major market for the films of "Mr. Kiss Kiss, Bang Bang," as he was known there. Bond, indeed, was a celebrity in Japan, which caused Connery, who did not want to be on public show all the time, some irritation. The film, lengthy but well sustained, again presented SPECTRE as trying to exploit the Cold War, but, unlike *From Russia, With Love* where Britain and the Soviet Union were the players, this story involved the United States and the Soviet Union. This was necessarily so; Blofeld's rocket, launched from his secret base in Japan (of which the Japanese knew nothing), was intercepting space missions. As only the United States and the Soviet Union had such a capacity, Britain was reduced to acting as a would-be mediator seeking to prevent the other two going to war. This, however, gives Britain a role, underlined by the information provided by a British tracking station and by the introduction of Bond at the outset in British-ruled Hong Kong, where the Royal Navy is shown as having an appreciable presence.

Ironically, this was the period in which Britain actually decided to disengage militarily from east of Suez, a disengagement that was to leave Hong Kong a total anachronism. This disengagement was in contrast with high hopes of continued regional potency held as recently as the coming to power of Harold Wilson as prime minister in 1964. However, the repeated financial crises of subsequent years, and notably 1966 and 1967, led to a major drawing in of international commitments, and not least as the Labour government was more concerned with social welfare expenditure. The 1960s were certainly not a unit in foreign policy or military proficiency, and this provided a shifting background to the Bond films. The government decided in February 1966 not to continue with plans for a new large aircraft carrier, which was to have been a major aspect of Britain's continued Indian Ocean presence, and followed by announcing, in January 1968, the rapid winding down of regional military bases in Singapore, the Persian Gulf, and Aden. The "East of Suez" policy was to be jettisoned. This represented not only a significant change in Britain's global military presence but also in the relationship with the United States, also seen in the determination, despite strong pressure from President Johnson, not to send troops to take part in the Vietnam War.

Villainy in *You Only Live Twice* has a Fu-Manchu touch, but a modern one. SPECTRE controls Japan's Osato Chemicals. It is being supplied with rocketry by China (on the pattern of the novel *Colonel Sun*), which is paying to cause war. Bond therefore saves the world from a nuclear cataclysm. The contrast with the plot of the novel was clear. There was none of the lassitude on Blofeld's part seen in that work or of the fascination with death and cultural decay. Instead, the engagement was with the present. This was shown in part by moving Blofeld from the samurai outfit and sword he uses in the novel. Ken Adam created an enormous, and expensive, set within the volcano that is Blofeld's base, a set with a monorail, elevators, and a full-sized rocket, ready for battle and where a dramatic battle is staged. The director of photography, Freddie Young, achieved some great shots, notably the aerial views for the fight on the roof of Osato's factory in Kobe.

The film is also strong on gadgets, most prominently "Little Nellie," an autogyro that enables Bond to do battle with SPECTRE helicopters; it is equipped with heat-seeking missiles, flame guns, rocket launchers, machine guns, smoke ejectors, and aerial mines. This was a version of the Aston Martin in *Goldfinger*, although it did not have the impact of that car. The powerful magnet carried by a Japanese secret service helicopter also enjoyed public interest; it was strong enough to lift a villain's car from Tokyo and drop it into Tokyo Bay.

The year 1967 was busy for films, not least with Connery's brother Neil in the seriously undistinguished *Operation Kid Brother*. The third of the Len Deighton/Harry Palmer films, *Billion Dollar Brain*, appeared. It was also the weakest of the three, and, indeed, a poor Bond substitute. That ended the series, which helped enable Bond to dominate the image of the spy. Despite having Richard Burton as the lead, John Le Carré's *The Spy Who Came in from the Cold* (1965), did not do well at the box office.

The American alternative, Dean Martin as Matt Helm in *The Silencers*, *Murderer's Row*, *The Ambushers*, and *The Wrecking Crew*, a series that appeared from 1966 to 1968, did not work well; Dean Martin was not a convincing adventure hero of the Connery type, however much he was up to the dialogue and dames part. *In Like Flint* (1967) was the ridiculous sequel to the more Bond-like *Our Man Flint* (1965), and James Coburn's challenge for the role ended. A more convincing rival appeared on television, *The Man from U.N.C.L.E.* (1964–1968), with a series of spin-off films. This oeuvre developed a market that Bond was best able to satisfy.

Broccoli meanwhile took Fleming in a different direction, producing in 1968 a film version of *Chitty Chitty Bang Bang*, written by Roald Dahl, the writer of *You Only Live Twice*. There were other debts to the Bond films, including the use of the actor Gert Fröbe, who had played Goldfinger.

Fed up with the pressure of publicity, and resenting what he saw as slights in his treatment by Eon, Connery then stepped aside to pursue alternative roles, leaving George Lazenby, "the different Bond from the same stable," according to the publicity, to star opposite Diana Rigg, a superb Bond girl, in *On Her Majesty's Secret Service*, which had its premiere in London on December 18, 1969. The idea of Bond having plastic surgery to explain the change was dropped. Effectively directed by Peter Hunt, who was the editor of the earlier films, the film had a brilliant villain, the American Telly Savalas, as a very physical and threatening Blofeld, superb ski chases, a good setting, notably Piz Gloria, the revolving restaurant near Murren in the Swiss Alps, and excellent music. It also worked as a love story, with Louis Armstrong singing "All the Time in the World." Indeed, the trailer advertised, "This one's different. This one's got heart."

Again, the world is at risk, with Blofeld able to use blackmail because the virus he has developed can produce total infertility in plants and animals: he will destroy all living things. Bond penetrates his alpine lair, the Institute for Allergy Research, masquerading as a figure from Britain's past, a herald devising a coat of arms for the vain Blofeld, and gains an insight into Blofeld's goals and methods, before being exposed. He has to flee in one of the most suspenseful sequences in a Bond film, in which action, photography, and music are brilliantly coordinated.

The United Nations is the body with which Blofeld, the head of a nongovernment organization, is negotiating; but, against orders, Bond intervenes in order to rescue Tracy, the brave Bond girl, whom he has already saved from suicide at the outset of the film. Bond is helped by Tracy's father, Marc-Ange Draco, the head of the Union Corse network of French criminals, who are presented as reasonable villains, unlike the world-grasping Blofeld. Indeed, Bond's ability, thanks to his resilience, personality, and bravery, to win such support is important to his effectiveness. However, the film, the longest at that stage, did not do well financially, grossing $64.6 million, only just over half the money taken for *You Only Live Twice* and less than half that for *Thunderball*. American cinema admission figures were only sixteen million.

These results contributed to disenchantment with Lazenby, who was not seen to be as effective as Connery. He certainly lacked the latter's ability to communicate menace. Lazenby's inexperience also proved a problem in the filming, and encouraged an emphasis on action rather than on the dialogue. He was certainly not brilliant but was overly sure of himself. Indeed, Lazenby's relations with the other stars were less than satisfactory. Lazenby also said he would not do another film. Furthermore, there were practical problems with scenes in Switzerland, including snowmelt, the failure to produce an avalanche on demand, and accidents. Many now consider the film to be one of the best; such was the impact of Roger Moore's subsequent portrayal. However, at the time, concern about actors and takings brought to a fore the more general issue of whether Bond was still working and viable. The next film would appear in the 1970s. What that would mean for a film franchise that started in the early 1960s was unclear, and not least because such franchises were relatively uncommon.

In *Diamonds Are Forever*, which opened in the United States on December 17, 1971, and in London on the 30th, Connery, who was still convincing as Bond, was persuaded to return, in return for a large fee that he gave to the Scottish International Education Trust. United Artists had turned down the director Guy Hamilton's suggestion for the part, Burt Reynolds. Initially, the diamonds theme was intended by the screenwriter, Richard Maibaum, as a hook to re-create the drama of *Goldfinger*, with Gert Fröbe, the actor who played the villain of that film, returning as a twin of Goldfinger who was to be fixated on diamonds, only to fall foul of Bond and Las Vegas. Broccoli rejected the idea and turned, instead, to Blofeld as the villain, and space, very topically, as a theme. This was another world-saver, with the diamond smuggling that was the target in the novel now intended, much more dramatically, to power the solar panels of the orbiting laser with which Blofeld is to launch world blackmail. The destruction of American, Chinese, and Soviet weaponry by the laser is shown: Blofeld's laser is literally above the Cold War, and is far more deadly and immediate than the threat to America supposedly presented by North Vietnam and the Viet Cong. Indeed, Blofeld sees himself as more powerful than "The Great Powers flexing their muscles like so many impotent beach boys," one of the many memorable lines from the film. Blofeld was the "non-state actor" with a vengeance.

The film very much focuses on America, indeed much more so than *Goldfinger*. Blofeld's wealth derives from kidnapping Willard Whyte, a reclusive Las Vegas–based billionaire, modeled on Howard Hughes, and taking over his empire. Much of the action was set in, or near, Las Vegas, a city of fabled opulence, which British viewers knew little about. Most of the supporting cast was American, as was much of the humor, as with the undertaker, Morton Slumber; and, with the exception of Bond, Britain plays only a peripheral role in the plot. Indeed, Blofeld brilliantly mocks Britain's inconsequence. He does not need to destroy British weaponry.

The Bond format was now well established as a clear production strategy. The filmic Bond varied in tone (and actor), but, with the camera as narrator, Bond was seen from outside. The paucity of reflective passages offered by the screen character and the emphasis on Bond as action hero aided this process. Politics and plot must provide a situation in which it is both legitimate and necessary to kill. There could be no ambivalence about this, because it would threaten public approval of Bond's exploits. Anchored in the world of good and bad, with Bond as the unerring nemesis for villains, the Bond world was totally at variance with the cultural relativism that became dominant in Western public ideology from the 1960s.

The Bond world, with its dark glamor, required a politics of conviction, specifically the notion of the British Secret Service as a benign force. Notably as played by Bernard Lee, a highly experienced actor who exemplified integrity, M must be authoritative as well as authoritarian, his analysis of the situation fair as well as accurate, Bond's mission necessary as well as legitimate. This differentiated the Bond world from those of Len Deighton and John Le Carré, in both of which betrayal, and, crucially, within the Secret Service, were central to plot and atmosphere and to a lack of confidence in the West, as well as being crucial to the methods of the Soviet Union.

Bond was also characterized by unflappable competence. Style meant competence, and competence ensured style. Competence was enhanced by presence, the presence reinforced by the much-detailed accoutrements and accessories of the Bond persona, and all in striking contrast to a public culture in which competence, style, rectitude, and duty were no longer regarded as absolutes and were increasingly denigrated by intellectuals and commentators. Bond indeed matched the role of lawman in the very moral Westerns of the period.

In contrast to Bond, Charles Gray as the cowardly Blofeld in the film *Diamonds Are Forever* was willing to have himself replicated through plastic surgery, to use a voice box to disguise his voice, and to escape from Las Vegas dressed as a woman, a disguise that threw off the gullible CIA, unlike Bond at the start of *Thunderball*. With Blofeld in *Diamonds Are Forever*, malleability was therefore linked to deceit. Blofeld is backed by murderous homosexual henchmen, Wint and Kidd, and by the lesbians Bambi and Thumper.

Integrity was clear in the films. It included aspects of behavior and views on appearance, different to those of today. The scene of British intelligence experts in *From Russia, With Love*, listening in London to Bond's radio report about the Lektor decoder, is a scene of ostentatious conventional masculinity: uniforms and cigarettes. No beards, baldness, or long hair are in sight.

There was also an element of continuity in the villains because of the use of SPECTRE and the character of Blofeld, albeit a Blofeld played by a series of actors. For example, Blofeld was shown as wearing Chairman Mao–style tunics, both in *You Only Live Twice* and in *Diamonds Are Forever*. This provided a visual display of villainy, and therefore it was not necessary to establish the plot by means of the device of the lengthy information-rich background used in the novels, each of which had a distinct plot.

The costs of filmmaking went up, in large part due to settings, special effects, and salaries, although inflation also played a role. Whereas just over $1 million was spent on *From Russia, With Love, Diamonds Are Forever* cost $7.2 million. However, the film was highly profitable, earning $15.6 million in the first twelve days of its release, and, with the comparative figures adjusted for inflation, had a worldwide gross of $116 million and American admissions of 26.5 million. The American settings doubtless helped with profitability. *Thunderball* was the most successful film at the American box office in 1966, whereas, although *You Only Live Twice* grossed $111.6 million, it was not as successful as *Thunderball*, in part because Japan was more remote in every sense. The films helped the novels. By 1973, twenty-six million copies of Fleming's Bond books had been sold in paperback by Pan alone.

With these returns for a clear format, the Bond films appeared set for a secure financial future. Moreover, there was a predictability that the audience liked, which made it far easier to obtain responses, strike echoes, and establish a self-referential world within which the rituals of a developing series were strong. The actor could be varied (on a very different pattern to the different Blofelds), but Bond was the star and was always at the center of the film. This meant that there was confidence about the need to replace Connery, but also about the value of doing so. Later commentators frequently discussed the identity of the best Bond, and the usual view was and is that Connery is the answer. In one sense, this is a helpful process, engaging as it does popular interest, but it is also misleading. These were and are all actors playing Bond, and Bond is the star. Indeed, this represents a success that is necessary for the franchise. This success also puts Bond on a level with Sherlock Holmes or Hercule Poirot, leaving them all very different from those characters who were indeed heavily dependent on one actor.

Comparison with Holmes is instructive as he is often depicted in terms of visual and stylistic indicators, notably his pipe, his deerstalker, his relationship with Dr. Watson, and his characteristic phrases. For Bond there are equivalents, particularly the vodka martini, shaken, not stirred, but the character is less dependent on individual tics. Instead, there are the more general preferences, especially for cars, women, and quips, and there is public interest in seeing how these will manifest themselves in particular stories and notably with the special effects. This interest carries forward into how individual actors have presented, and will present, these aspects of Bond.

5

MOORE AND AMERICANIZATION

The year 1983 saw it all. There were two Bond films, but there was also the near breakout of World War III, with the seconds ticking away in a fashion straight out of one of the films. On September 26, 1983, the Soviet early-warning system reported first the launch of an American missile from Montana and, subsequently, a large-scale attack. Fortunately, the reports were treated as false alarms by Stanislav Petrov, the deputy chief for algorithms, and the Soviets did not launch their own missiles. Roger Moore was the somewhat unlikely defender of the West at this juncture. In common with the films, however, split-second timing was the order of the day, and it was only accidentally that we all survived the year. Half of everything was and is luck.

A Bond who is not honored much in retrospect, although he has many fans, Moore in practice carried the part for a sequence of seven films and for thirteen years, which was more than Connery had done when Moore took over the role in 1973, although Connery came back, for one film only, in 1983. Moore was already a star before he became Bond. He was famous, not only in Britain but also in important foreign markets such as West Germany, for his television role as Simon Templar. After the relatively unknown Connery and the completely unknown Lazenby, the choice of Moore was a good move; the new Bond was known and would bring fans with him. The television roles he had played were in a way very similar to that of Bond. After the relatively innovative *On Her Majesty's Secret Service* and what seemed the last Connery in *Diamonds Are Forever*, the producer wanted a "safe" film, with a known actor as Bond.

The epithets frequently flung at Moore were not complimentary: stagy, formulaic, jokey, unthreatening, old. In every case, he is contrasted with Connery. It is therefore arresting to reexamine the first of the Moore films, *Live and Let Die* (1973). Directed by Guy Hamilton and written by Tom Mankiewicz, this is a work with considerable energy, an effective villain, good fights, an amazing speedboat chase in Louisiana (with a jet-propulsion device fitted to one boat), and interesting settings. Better in some respects than the novel, the film again played into American anxieties, although without threatening the future of the world. Losing in Indochina, although that is never mentioned in the film, America now had to look to its own defenses.

The plot offered a menace to offset the jokiness of many of the lines as well as of the farcical Sheriff J. W. Pepper character. This kind of character was a standard in American comedies, as in *Smokey and the Bandit* (1977) and Sam Peckinpah's *Convoy* (1978). The threat was to the United States, with the Mr. Big of New York African American crime aiming to drive out the Mafia by providing free heroin, to increase the number of drug addicts, and then, having cornered the market, to push up prices. Without a Chinese presence, this is another version of *Goldfinger* to that extent—one of crime as monopoly. It is not, however, a plan for nuclear cataclysm. Harlem, Mr. Big's base, is presented as menacing, with part of it a grim wasteland where Bond, who does not understand the term, is to be "wasted" by gangsters who laugh at his foppishness. Subliminally as well as in sledgehammer terms, this is about fears of black power, the cities, and crime, and drew on the Watts riots in Los Angeles in 1965, those in Detroit in 1967, and other less prominent riots. The threat to the United States is given a different menace to that in the 1954 novel of the same name because the Mr. Big of African American crime is not, in the novel, a creature of the Cold War, which was a fear Fleming took from the anxieties of his contemporaries such as J. Edgar Hoover, the head of the FBI.

Instead, Mr. Big is really Dr. Kananga. This is the McGuffin of the plot that Bond eventually uncovers, in the detection that is so significant to the stories. The president of San Monique, an imaginary Caribbean state, Kananga is able to use a rubber face mask to adopt his New York persona. The plot could draw on the popularity in the early 1970s, at least in the United States in large cities, of Blaxploitation films. A large part of the Mr. Big character was taken from those films, and thus *Live and Let Die* could try to break into the audience that was watching those films.

In what is a harsh depiction of Caribbean independence, there is much made of the role of voodoo, in both tone and plot. The implication is that Western power is required in order to maintain control and free the people from the subjugation based on their fears. If Western imperialism appears to be the answer, there is also implicit criticism of the United Nations, which Kananga uses as a sounding board to denounce the West, employing the sort of language directed at the United States in the era of the Vietnam War. This was a film very much located on the Western side of the Cold War.

Moreover, the theme of African American menace is taken forward by the somewhat obsessive account of Kananga's would-be ownership of his tarot reader, the virginal, white Solitaire. Solitaire and her tarot reading are a reference to the 1960s and early-1970s obsession with the occult. She was played, in a somewhat weak fashion, by Jane Seymour in a sort of naïve allurement that was a tribute to late-1960s alternative life but also a talisman of white fears about black sexuality. Bond and Kananga are rivals for her affection. By seducing her, Bond gains ascendancy over his sadistic opponent, although with his threat to have his finger cut off by his heavy, Tee Hee, Kananga then comes as close as family entertainment allows to suggesting that he will be emasculated. Initially the Solitaire role had been intended for an African American actress, but United Artists had insisted on a white one.

The film still leaves a very uncomfortable feel, in its treatment of Solitaire and in its racism, both in New York and in the Caribbean. In a film with many African Americans in it, only two are good, and one is murdered by the agents of Mr. Big, while most are evil or foolish. However, there is no doubt of the film's energy. The emphasis on voodoo and tarot, at once sinister but also mocking, enables the film to play with ideas of mystery and chance, providing an extra dimension to the story as well as underlining the strange exotic world Bond has to master. This emphasis is seen from the killing of three British agents at the outset, one while observing a New Orleans funeral that turns out to be his own, and on to the very end when Baron Samedi, a menacing voodoo figure, appears on the locomotive at the front of the train carrying Bond. This is exoticism in America and a very different United States to *Goldfinger* and *Diamonds Are Forever*.

There was no doubt of Moore's charisma in his new role. He started into the role with all engines running. The Moore formula and style were there from the first film. Moore was more stagy than Connery, as well as an elegant cigar-smoking gent, in a more upper-class reading than that of Connery. Linked to the staginess there were jokey sequences, notably the farcical bus chase in San Monique, in which the police are thwarted by Bond driving a London-style bus, and also Bond cheating at cards when seducing Solitaire. Much of the audience found this acceptable. Connery's Bond would probably not have bothered with cheating.

A certain amount of the film involved tropes, variations of the same theme, a pattern frequently seen with the Bond films. It is as if a Bond film is like a very good meal that you already know and love. Had once in a while, it is very tasty, with some variants in the cooking, but always on a familiar pattern. In *Live and Let Die* this was particularly the case at the close when Bond fights the villain's enforcer Tee Hee on the train, a reprise of the scene on the Orient Express in *From Russia, With Love*. There were also numerous similarities with *Dr. No*. These included, as part of its Caribbean menace, the villains trying to kill Bond in his hotel room with a poisonous creature. On the other hand, the sharks of *Thunderball* are replaced by crocodiles, providing Bond with opportunities for a dramatic escape from the crocodile farm, which involves humor not seen with the sharks.

Moreover, the settings in Louisiana and New York are new for the Bond films, while the music was transformed for the film. The first Bond film not to have its music made by John Barry, it had instead a sure-fire title song by Paul McCartney and his wife Linda. Composed by George Martin, the "fifth Beatle" who was their "director," the song reached number two on the American charts, and was the first Bond theme nominated for an Academy Award. Adjusted for inflation, the film grossed $126.4 million, more than any hitherto bar *Thunderball*, although the American admissions fell to 20.1 million.

Moore had been offered a three-picture deal by United Artists, and this film suggested that they had been correct. He was easier to take than George Lazenby. A very different locale was offered in *The Man with the Golden Gun* (1974), in which the focus was not on the United States, despite the emphasis in the novel on America as the target. The Cold War is not to the fore. Appropriately, given the 1973 oil crisis, a crisis of limited availability and far greater cost, the politics of the film instead focused on energy, although this focus was really an enabler for the duel between

Bond and Scaramanga, the world's most expensive assassin. Solar energy is the key theme, with Scaramanga discovering, with the Solex technology, the secret of how to use it, both to generate power and as a weapon. The Chinese are a presence; they shelter Scaramanga, and the film was set in Macao, Hong Kong, Bangkok, and on the Chinese (in fact Thai) coast. Scaramanga seeks to trick the Chinese. Having, on their behalf, sought the Solex Agitator, he takes it for himself in order to stage an auction. Similarly, he is a KGB assassin who had gone freelance, prefiguring the idea of Soviet rogue agents also seen in *Octopussy* and *A View to a Kill*.

Scaramanga also has a third nipple, which is reputedly an indicator of sexual prowess and invulnerability. This sexuality is linked to a perversity, in the shape of an association of personality and sexuality with his gun. Scaramanga is a case of the villain again as a vain egomaniac, but one with his personality far more linked with his sexuality than previous villains, notably Blofeld.

Bond is not a comparable figure of menace, and the absence of Connery was particularly notable here. Indeed, M's complaint about Bond's impact—"Jealous husbands, outraged chefs, humiliated tailors"—scarcely matches the sinister poise of the villain. Somewhat fancifully, Scaramanga says that he and Bond are the same—"ours is the loneliest profession"—and that they both gain fulfillment from killing. Bond, however, sees himself as vindicated by his missions: "When I kill it's on the specific orders of my government, and those I kill are themselves killers."

The somewhat hurried film had a very offhand attitude to women, notably Mary Goodnight, but Christopher Lee, a stepcousin of Fleming's, provided an arresting portrayal of the villain. The gadgets and stunts were impressive, notably a somersaulting car, as well as a car that becomes an aircraft, which was based on a vehicle that was a Ford Pinto with added Cessna parts. There was also a golden gun that was readily assembled by the villain from a pen, lighter, and cigarette case, although the rocket-firing camera was cut. Scaramanga's house is a spooky gun park, a shooting gallery based on optical illusion and with automated marionettes. A comic element was offered by Nick Nack, his dwarf sidekick played by the three-foot-eleven-inch-tall French actor Hervé Villechaize. Yet, the film does not work in the end. Indeed, the weak close has the feel of an afterthought.

A more immediate threat to the world was posed in *The Spy Who Loved Me* (1977), the first Bond film for which Broccoli was sole producer, the first Bond film recorded in Dolby Surround Stereo, and one that broke the record for gross earnings. Broccoli and Saltzman had fallen out and Saltzman had sold his share to Broccoli. By 1977, the West appeared in chaos. This was a West struggling to recover from the economic crisis linked to the 1973 oil price surge, from failure in Vietnam and the Watergate crisis in the United States, and from the 1974 miners' strike and 1976 IMF crisis in Britain.

In the film, a rather different plutocrat, in the shape of Karl Stromberg, the first real megalomaniacal villain, wishes to destroy the world and to build a new civilization under the sea controlled from Atlantis, his submersible Mediterranean base. This was an impressive *Thunderbirds*-style villains' base, and something straight out of a comic book, for example, the "Nick Fury, agent of Shield" series from Marvel Comics in 1966–1967, which was the Marvel answer to the Bond films.

To achieve his goal, Stromberg seizes a British and a Soviet nuclear submarine, holding them captive in a supertanker with an opening bow. These submarines are programmed to fire missiles at New York and Moscow, in order to launch a nuclear holocaust of modern civilization, which Stromberg, on the theme of Blofeld in the novel *You Only Live Twice*, describes as corrupt and decadent. In contrast to Blofeld, Stromberg is a public figure who owns a legitimate company. His drive to destroy is different from that of Blofeld; the latter sought to dominate the world. In place of Blofeld and SPECTRE, however, Broccoli created two different types of more dramatic Blofeld for this and the following film.

This was a period of marked confrontation between American and Soviet fleets, focused on submarines and their ballistic missiles. Over three-quarters of Soviet naval expenditure was on the submarine force. This threat obliged NATO powers to develop patrol areas for their submarines, and both sides focused on surveillance.

Bond saves the world by searching for the heat-signature tracking device that enabled Stromberg to follow and successfully intercept the submarines. This search takes him to Egypt, where much of the action was set in exotic locales, and then to Sardinia, close to Atlantis. The real enemy is not the Soviet Union and, indeed, these were years when détente between West and East was to the fore.

The film was most memorable for its opening sequence, set in the Alps, in which Bond escapes pursuing Soviet assassins by skiing off the slopes into a freefall in a deep valley. A parachute appears and is released, with the Union Jack on its canopy opening up, the hero is saved, the audience astounded (some early audiences cheered and the scene is still impressive on repeated viewing), and the story kicks off. Having thus escaped assassination by this skiing Soviet hit team, Bond is then instructed to work with the Soviets, and specifically with the girlfriend of the head of the hit team whom Bond has killed at the outset. She vows to kill him, but they fall for each other after an on-off romance that has echoes of Hollywood comedies.

In this adventure, there was a clear fantasy element, not least with Stromberg's assassin, Jaws, with his steel-capped teeth. Bond's submersible Lotus Esprit sports car, able to fire a rocket capable of shooting down a helicopter, was an effective fantasy weapon. It was produced as a toy car like the Aston Martin in

Goldfinger. There was also a memorable set, supposedly the inside of Stromberg's ship, for the big fight at the close.

There was no reference in the Egypt section either to East-West or regional tensions in the Middle East or in the Horn of Africa where, in August 1977, Soviet-armed Somalia attacked Ethiopia.

Moonraker (1979), again proposed a threat to the world. Drax, another stand-alone mega-capitalist villain rather than a member of SPECTRE, intends to create a master race in space based on his space station and to destroy the rest of the species by firing nerve gas back at the Earth. The plot was a response to the popular market revealed in the enormous success of *Star Wars* (1977) and *Close Encounters of the Third Kind* (1978). This response required money, lots of it, in part for the special effects and sets. *For Your Eyes Only* had been due to succeed *The Spy Who Loved Me*, but *Moonraker*, with its space theme, replaced it. Replaced it, but with a totally different plot to the novel aside from the villain's name and a short scene, found near the close, of hero and villain imprisoned beneath a rocket in order to be the victims of its launch. The film was a boost to the public awareness of the American Space Shuttle program. It showed a shuttle launch years before the real first one. The master race scenario had deliberate echoes of the Nazis. Played by Michael Lonsdale, Drax, however, is creepy rather than menacing, and certainly lacks the energy of the Drax of the novel. The villains as well as Bond had become stagy. *Moonraker*, like *The Spy Who Loved Me* and *You Only Live Twice*, was directed by Lewis Gilbert and there were many similarities between them, not least in their concern with rocketry and space, although that was also a theme of other films, especially *Diamonds Are Forever*.

Costing $34 million to make, as much as the first eight Bond films together, and filmed in France due to tax problems in Britain, *Moonraker* broke box-office records for a Bond film, with a worldwide gross of $202.7 million and an American audience of 25.5 million. Its popularity reflected the appeal of space at the time of *Star Wars*, but also it was a very easy watch. The audience was pleased, not least with the return, in response to a public letter-writing campaign, of Jaws, now a cult figure. The settings, notably in Brazil, were exotic. The drama was clear: Bond at the outset left an aircraft without a parachute in a freefall jump, a sequence that required much practice, and also went into space for the first time. North American critics lavishly praised the film, notably Vincent Canby of the *New York Times*, Jay Scott of Canada's *Globe and Mail*, and Lawrence O'Toole of *Maclean's Magazine*. *Moonraker* was nominated for an Oscar for its special effects, one of the few Oscar nominations for a Bond film, but lost out to *Alien*. However, the script lacked bite and the female lead, Lois Chiles as Holly Goodhead, was of scant interest.

The next film, *For Your Eyes Only* (1981), was far less cataclysmic in plot, or melodramatic in tone, and also was poorly received and took in far less money. The film, which is completely set in Europe, drew heavily on the twist of the plot of Fleming's short story "Risico." Space plays no role and nor do sharks, but skiing, instead, is restored to prominence. After the pre-title sequence in which Bond thwarts an assassination attempt and drops a Blofeld lookalike down a chimney, the Cold War is present in the struggle to thwart the Soviet Union from gaining control of an ATAC (Automatic Targeting Attack Communicator) transmitter that is employed to instruct British submarines to fire ballistic missiles. The Mediterranean, with excursions inland in Spain, Italy, and Greece, provides the setting. There is neither the exotic appeal of the Orient nor the glamor of the Caribbean, nor the interest or menace offered to Americans by a setting in the New World. Greece was a more mundane holiday destination for Europeans and was not one with which most Americans were familiar.

There is the very marked difference in personality between East and West, with Eric Kriegler, a KGB agent who is a killer, presented as a fanatic who eats only health foods and will not talk to women. However, détente is offered at the end when Bond destroys the ATAC, telling the KGB's General Gogol that neither of them having the machine is détente. Of course, as the ATAC is a British device, the British have many more. Gogol himself looks like a good old uncle and appears reasonable. The film made no reference to the markedly deteriorating international situation. The pro-Western Shah had been overthrown in Iran in the winter of 1978–1979 and the American embassy in Tehran was seized by student radicals in November 1979, while, in December 1979, Soviet forces had occupied Afghanistan.

In a comic ending to *For Your Eyes Only*, a parrot pretending to be Bond asks Margaret Thatcher, the British prime minister, who has telephoned to congratulate him, for a kiss. The following year, she was to send a task force to recapture the Falklands from an Argentinean invasion force.

In *Octopussy* (1983), the Cold War comes to the fore anew. In an early draft, the story involved Blofeld, who murders M, takes control of MI6 with a mole M, fires Moneypenny, and has Bond branded as a double agent. Bond goes to Afghanistan to fight, alongside Kamal Khan and Octopussy, against the Soviet Union in order to clear his name and stop Blofeld. In the event, there was a more conventional theme of Soviet aggression, albeit with the interesting variant that it is a rogue element among the Soviets, one General Orlov, who is the cause of the crisis. General Gogol is a goody, and Orlov has to circumvent the Soviet system in his zeal to attack the West.

Ironically, in 1982–1983, the Cold War, indeed, came to a new height with the Soviet Union considering an attack on Western Europe. Far from being a rogue element, this was a Soviet Union in which Yuri Andropov, the Soviet leader from 1982 to 1984, was both paranoid and willing to plan a war in response to what the KGB repeatedly, but inaccurately, reported was an imminent Western attack. The rhetoric of conflict had greatly increased with Ronald Reagan, who was elected US president in 1980. In June 1982, he called for a "crusade for freedom," and in March 1983 referred to the Soviet Union as an "evil empire." Reagan outlined later in March the need for a "Star Wars" program, or Strategic Defense Initiative, which would enable the United States to dominate space, employing space-mounted weapons (as in *Diamonds Are Forever*) to destroy Soviet satellites and missiles.

In response to the Reaganite military buildup, the Soviet Union, with its anxious leadership fed intelligence reports from the KGB about American plans for a surprise nuclear first strike, adopted an aggressive pose. The Soviets further built up their navy, with the laying down of a carrier, the *Admiral Kuznetsov*, in 1982 and, most notably, with the *Typhoon* class of ballistic missile submarines. They could remain under the sanctuary of the Arctic ice cap and then surface just at the edge of it, fire their missiles, and rapidly retreat under the ice. In 1983, the deployment of cruise and Pershing missiles in Western Europe excited Soviet concern and anger. The Soviets feared attack under the cover of Able Archer, a NATO military exercise held that November to test nuclear attack procedures. In the event, the Americans scaled down Able Archer and, in terms of active hostilities, restricted themselves to conquering the Caribbean island of Grenada in October in order to prevent it from becoming another Cuba.

The plot of *Octopussy* ranged to South Asia, with Bond sent to India for the first time. That offered a fantasy element, notably with elephants, beautiful women, a princely fort, and balloon-borne attackers. The chaotic street chase left no cliché untouched, although Bond's Indian assistant was shown as capable of handling the situation. The villain, Kamal Khan, was an exiled Afghan prince. Together with the non-Indians Octopussy and

Bond, this ensured that Indians were only helpers for the non-Indian characters. There were very few Indian women among Octopussy's group. Kamal Khan was a leftover from the first draft, although the Afghan-Soviet conflict was dropped from the plot, only to reappear in *The Living Daylights* (1987).

The depiction of India in *Octopussy*, not so much the luxury of the famous Lake Palace Hotel in Udaipur, as in the street scenes and the hunt, is far more fantastical than that of Europe or America when they appear in the films. This element of fantasy was taken much further with an all-female smuggling network headed by Octopussy, and by the cover for the smuggling offered by a circus that includes Mischka and Grischka, homicidal twin knife-throwers, who are agents for the rogue Soviet marshal. The all-female Octopussy group, based on its lavish barge, was totally implausible, and helped make the film ridiculous. Maud Adams as Octopussy was the first woman who was not in the employment of the villain, and was richer and more powerful than Kamal Khan. The fight on top of an aircraft was implausible as well, although the incredible aircraft in the pre-title sequence set in Cuba was a real-life Acrostar. The global gross takings were $183,700,000 and the American audience 25.5 million. The film was received in the United States better than usual for a Bond film.

The same year saw the appearance of *Never Say Never Again*. Not produced by Eon, this vehicle for Connery provided a reprise of *Thunderball* (1965). Whereas that film involved the theft of a British atomic bomber, the greater salience of the United States was shown by the plot now centering on the theft, again from Britain, of two American cruise missiles. One is to be positioned by SPECTRE underneath the White House, the other to threaten Middle Eastern oil production, and both are to be detonated if a ransom demand is not met. This is the apparently real version of Largo's pain-inducing game "Domination," which he obliges

Bond to play, only to lose to Bond. The film was an American product, with an American director (Irvin Kershner), writer (Lorenzo Semple), and special effects head (John Dykstra). The director of photography, however, Douglas Slocombe, was British.

As in *Thunderball*, Largo from SPECTRE was the villain, although the Mediterranean, not the Caribbean, was his boat background in this film. The Mediterranean enables a setting in Monte Carlo, with a plot move to North Africa. The sadistic killing of a female British agent helps establish the villainy of the baddies. Klaus Maria Brandauer, who played Largo, was an excellent baddie, a psychopath with terrifying mood swings, and Kim Basinger as Domino was a fine female lead, indeed a better one than in the films since *Diamonds Are Forever*.

The villain's number two was Fatima Blush, SPECTRE No. 12, played by Barbara Carrera. She was one of the most impressive in a line of Bond female villains, and was to be reprised in part by Xenia Onatopp in *GoldenEye*. These women are very different from a villainess such as Fiona Volpe in *Thunderball*. The last also was a fighter in bed, taking sexual voracity as a way to devour a willing male, but Fatima, like Xenia, is also a madly cruel killer, whereas Volpe is only an assassin. Fatima is joyful in getting the possibility of killing Bond and later Domino. Having captured Bond, she prepares to shoot him first in his penis, before deciding to make him write a note declaring that making love to Fatima was "the greatest pleasure of your life." After Bond's riposte, "Well, there was this girl in Philadelphia," a joke essentially for Americans, the episode leads to Fatima being killed by Bond's Union Jack pen and its armament of an exploding nib, although only after it was unclear whether the pen-gun worked.

Britain, nevertheless, appeared less and less relevant. In the film *Diamonds Are Forever* (1971), Blofeld had mocked Bond: "Surely you haven't come to negotiate, Mr. Bond. Your pitiful little island hasn't even been threatened." Eight years later, in the film *Moonraker*, Drax tells Bond, "your country's one indisputable contribution to world civilization [is] afternoon tea." In *Never Say Never Again*, the filmic reworking of *Thunderball*, the country was clearly going downhill, and not least as compared to the original. The porter at Shrublands greets Bond with the remark that they no longer made cars like his; the new M, dryly played by a reserved Edward Fox, distances himself from his predecessor and makes it clear that he has little use for the 00 section, which he sees as redundant. Instead, M is now tedious, health-obsessive, intent on purging toxins from the body. He warns against eating red meat. Alec McCowen as Q, Algernon in this film, complains of slashed budgets, dullness, and rule by bureaucrats and computers. Noting that Bond means "gratuitous sex and violence," he is openly envious of Bond going to the Caribbean.

Bond, a figure from the past, as he was played by Connery for the only time since 1971, has as his antithesis Nigel Small-Fawcett, a British diplomat in the West Indies, a prattish role brilliantly realized by Rowan Atkinson. The latter's pursuit of virtue takes the form of worrying that Bond will cause trouble, jeopardizing the tourist trade. This safety-first attitude, in fact, threatens the national interest. Bond is necessarily robust in ignoring it, but now his individualism is one opposed to the Establishment, instead of being delegated by it. This is a crucial shift. The hero is now truly an outsider. The Sixties has become political correctness, and Bond is left out on a limb. At the same time, Connery plays the part very well, and the plot is more interesting than those of many Bond films. The film lacked the music and other trademarks of the Eon Bonds, although a fan-cut of the film with John Barry music was produced.

Also in 1983, George Lazenby returned to offer a Bond-like portrayal in *The Return of the Man from U.N.C.L.E.* Connery went on in *The Rock* (1996) to play an imprisoned agent, John

Mason, like Bond. Mason is caught by the Americans stealing their biggest secrets, only to break out of Alcatraz and kill nearly half of the rogue American military unit that had taken over Alcatraz.

The last of the Moore films was *A View to a Kill* (1985), a film produced before the thawing of the Cold War that followed Mikhail Gorbachev coming to power in the Soviet Union that March. Indeed, when the film was being made a forceful struggle for primacy between the United States and the Soviet Union continued in several areas of the world, notably in Afghanistan, Angola, and Central America. *A View to a Kill* saw a villain bringing together the Cold War and the Nazis, as Fleming had done in his novel *Moonraker*, with the villain's objective being the cornering of the world microchip industry by means of the underground explosion of a bomb in a cave full of explosives in order to set off the San Andreas Fault and then destroy Silicon Valley with a massive flood. That was far more credible than the original idea of the villain forcing Halley's Comet to crash into the valley. Most of the action was set in California, including the dramatic denouement in an airship by the Golden Gate Bridge, although there was an important earlier section in France. The psychotic villain, Max Zorin, played by Christopher Walken, had not only menace, but also great energy and drive (as well as slimness) that Moore lacked. So also did Grace Jones, whose character, Mayday, was on the pattern of a villain's woman who comes to realize she has been cheated by the villain and who turns to the good. She takes the primary bomb out of the mine, thwarting Zorin, but it explodes, killing her.

Moore's depiction of the Bond character seemed out of place. This was a matter not only of Bond's easy sexuality and repartee, in the age first of women's emancipation and, then, of AIDS, but also of his demeanor. Dinner-jacketed heroes were out, as was the world of casinos. Style had changed and been democratized.

The stylish, gentlemanly conduct of Bond could now seem effete. The begrimed torso of Sylvester Stallone, as in *Rambo: First Blood Part II* (1985), now struck a more popular note. In addition, there was a lack of dramatic intensity in the plot of *A View to a Kill*, and the end had weaknesses. This was certainly not *Goldfinger*, even though the plot was very similar with Mayday playing the Pussy Galore part. The plot had the potential to be more menacing, as Zorin is the result of Nazi genetic manipulation, notably the testing of steroids on pregnant women, and is totally psychotic, eager to machine gun his own workers once he has no use for them. Tanya Roberts as Stacey Sutton, the female lead, was of no interest.

For Your Eyes Only (1981), *Octopussy* (1983), and *A View to a Kill* (1985), in each of which Moore played Bond with less energy, were poorly received, and the takings for each successively fell. The last had a worldwide gross of $152,627,960 and an American audience of 16.6 million compared to 25.5 million for *Octopussy*. Criticism of Moore rose and, as he recognized, he had become formulaic and way too old, as he was to say on the audio commentary that accompanied the Blu-rays of all but the last of the Moore Bonds. The Bond franchise badly needed rebooting and was frequently treated and presented in that light.

6

THE DALTON GLASNOST YEARS

In 1986, Eon settled on an established star to replace Moore. It was to be Pierce Brosnan, the thirty-three-year-old hero of an American television drama, NBC's *Remington Steele*. NBC had canceled the series, freeing the dynamic Brosnan for Bond. However, NBC then renewed the series, and Brosnan, who had been publicly proclaimed as the new choice, was contractually obliged to go on being Steele. Indeed, Brosnan was on the way to a press conference where he was to be presented as the new Bond when he got the call from the television producer. Instead of Brosnan, while others were mentioned, the choice was swiftly announced in August 1986. It was an unexpected one. Born in 1946, Timothy Dalton had auditioned for *On Her Majesty's Secret Service*, and in 1972 had been considered anew, only for Moore to be selected. Dalton was far from young.

The first idea was for a film about Bond's earlier mission, a story intended to show how a young naval officer became 007, but Broccoli thought the audience would not be interested in amateur days, although in *Casino Royale* the idea was deployed. This would have been a throwback film; moreover, it could not be expected to appeal to American audiences because the focus would be on midcentury Britain. Instead, the taut short story

"The Living Daylights" was used as the basis for the opening section of the plot, with lots of extraneous material then bolted on—material that did not really relate to it.

With Dalton, however, the Bond on screen most reflected Fleming's Bond, or, rather, the Bond of the 1950s. Dalton, a trained and experienced actor, but also not a person who was looking for the spotlight of publicity, was able to offer Bond as a seasoned agent but also a troubled Romantic hero, his self-sufficiency a burden as well as a badge of honor. This was very much Fleming's vision. Bond's tasks became morally complex missions. This was notably so in Dalton's second Bond film, *Licence to Kill* (1989). In this, Bond pursues the villain Sanchez for the latter's cruelty toward his old friend Leiter. Sanchez had Leiter fed to a shark, badly maiming him, while Leiter's new wife, Della, is killed after probably being raped by Sanchez's men. American anxieties about Hispanic men, their violence, unpredictability, cruelty, and sexuality, were well to the fore.

Whereas previous Bonds had been essentially facetious toward M, Bond was ready in this film to defy orders and to leave the service. This was despite being told by M that he could not do so, that MI6 was not like a country club from which one could resign, which was very much an American image, and that he must hand in his gun. Indeed, the film was originally to be called *Licence Revoked.* In *The Living Daylights* (1987), Bond was also ready to be sacked.

With Dalton there was an attempt to reset the franchise. He presented himself as taking on the true mantle: "I intend to approach this project with a sense of responsibility to the work of Ian Fleming." Broccoli, meanwhile, prepared to draw a link between Dalton and Connery. In practice, Dalton came across as more of a gentleman than Connery, and more charming, but not as conveying menace or humor as Connery had done. Indeed, Dalton's earnestness was largely humorless and his lack of humor brought little to the character. More positively, Dalton played Bond straight. As a very emotionally repressed Bond, he appeared to carry much emotion with him, which made him much more complex than the more freewheeling Moore.

Supporting *glasnost* (openness), Mikhail Gorbachev, who became Soviet leader in March 1985, sought to strengthen the Soviet Union and the Communist Party, but also pursued a less combative and confrontational international stance. Indeed, cooperation between the Soviet Union and Britain against Brad Whitaker, a rogue American arms dealer, was a theme in *The Living Daylights*, which appeared as the Cold War was easing even though it continued. More generally, the arms-and-drugs-dealing plot matched some of the realities on the ground in this period. Aside from Whitaker, there was also an untrustworthy Soviet general, Georgi Koskov, as well as Afghan guerrillas, under an Oxford-educated leader, Kamran Shah. These guerrillas align with Bond against the Soviets, assaulting a Soviet airbase in Afghanistan. This felt like a scene from David Lean's classic film *Lawrence of Arabia* (1962), with the Afghan leader like a bearded English gentleman. There were echoes of the early plans for *Octopussy*. This placing in Afghanistan was a reflection of the Cold War and, more particularly, of the successful Afghan resistance to Soviet occupation in 1979–1988. As a result, the film offered a moment of alliance that now appears peculiar if not incredible to most viewers, and, notably, American ones. This sense of dissociation is not one, however, that the filmmakers needed to worry about; their intended audience was looking at the film for the first time and when the film came out, not in retrospect. The continued popularity of the films, however, ensures that many do watch them in that fashion. So also with the dubious *Rambo III* (1988), where Rambo fights the Soviets in the Afghan mountains and frees his mentor, who had been captured by the Soviets while training the Afghans.

Some of the scenes in *The Living Daylights* worked very well, notably the attack by the killer Necros, as a pretend milkman, wielding explosive milk bottles, on Blaydon, a MI6 safe house. The film was the last Bond score by John Barry, and one of his best. However, the convoluted plot was full of ridiculous double-crosses: this was Le Carré without the suspense or setting. The updated Aston Martin Bond drove and used to escape from Czechoslovakia included ground-to-ground missiles, which were more deadly than the villains, who lacked a world-shaking master plan. Whitaker might praise Napoleon, and be killed by a bust of Wellington, but he commanded nothing serious. His praise of Hitler as cutting away "society's dead flesh" scarcely matched his limited potential. As such, the film was similar to *Live and Let Die* and *For Your Eyes Only* in that there was no "master plan" to bring down everything.

Licence to Kill was the most American Bond film, with no scene in Britain. Franz Sanchez, a sadistic drug king, offered a parallel to the theme of placelessness seen with SPECTRE and its willingness to extort from all. Based in a thinly disguised Panama, he is depositing much of his money in the United States. Sanchez takes American orders for drugs and sets the price under the cover of his employee, Professor Joe Butcher, who operates as a television evangelist seeking pledges (i.e., orders) over the television. Sanchez sees money as the universal solvent and it certainly works as such in "Isthmus," where it appears that everything and everybody can be bought. This is a prelude to the hostile depiction of Bolivia and its authorities in *Quantum of Solace* (2006).

In 1989, the United States invaded Panama to depose its drug-dealing dictator, General Manuel Noriega, who had a pock-marked face rather like that of Sanchez. The link would have been obvious to contemporaries, although the invasion itself occurred six months after the premiere. With the film, the public had a context within which to understand why America was apparently invading Panama. Sanchez is presented as a potent figure, owning "the world's largest private investment fund," and running "an invisible empire from Chile to Alaska." This is an aspect of the vulnerable underbelly theme. Sanchez is wanted in the United States on 139 felony counts and, on his shoulder, his far-from-cuddly pet is an iguana with a diamond-studded choker.

The Living Daylights and *Licence to Kill* were grittier in plot and tone than the Moore films. There was still a clear depiction of evil, but the forces of good were less sure. In *Licence to Kill*, there is a corrupt and treacherous American lawman (whom Bond eventually kills) who frees Sanchez, after Bond and Leiter have captured him, and thus is responsible for the attack on Leiter. Bond sends him to his death, but the American authorities are unwilling to act against Sanchez when he is outside American jurisdiction. Moreover, when Bond tells M that Leiter has risked his life for him, M cruelly retorts, "Spare me this sentimental rubbish." Q, however, comes to Bond's aid, bringing him a series of devices and acting as a field agent. This, again, was not credible, and reflected, instead, the retreading of familiar characters, already seen, in the Moore films, with Jaws.

Drugs and false religion are presented as sapping society, though the society in question is the United States, not a Britain where evangelicalism in practice was weak. In *Licence to Kill*, Bond confronts what would soon be termed the "death of history," for Sanchez is not interested in ideology, but simply in making money by dominating the American and Pacific drug markets. In a comic presentation that had not been seen earlier with SPECTRE, sacred space—Butcher's Meditation Institute—is a religious experience designed solely to act as a cover for the drug trade and for drug production. So also with the role of finance in the shape of Sanchez's yuppie accountant, Truman Lodge, who uses the language of marketing, only to be killed near the end by

Sanchez as an overhead that needs to be taken out of the equation. This was satire in a rather humorless film, not espionage or adventure.

Despite this, *Licence to Kill* was a very violent film with no holds barred, a product of the handling of violence on television and by the media more generally. The violence was a reflection of the often vicious action films of the period, such as *Die Hard* (1988) and the very violent Stallone and Schwarzenegger films. This violence affected the classification of *Licence to Kill* by the British Board of Film Classification which, indeed, insisted on some cuts for the British market. At the level of cruelty, there were no limits in this film. Sanchez has his henchman, Milton Krest, whom he distrusts, explode inside a decompression chamber, while another figure who displeases him by having a relationship with Sanchez's lover has his heart cut out. Sanchez's henchmen are also vicious, including Dario, who "used to be with the Contras till they kicked him out." The special effects were dramatic, including the burning to death of Sanchez at the end of a successful pursuit of petroleum tankers by one that had been commandeered by Bond. This was special effects with a vengeance, and, indeed, was highly dangerous.

Many modern viewers do not recall the Dalton films with much pleasure, which is disappointing; he was a good actor and the scripting was reasonable. Nevertheless, Dalton did not, possibly could not, live the part. As there was no sequel until 1995, Dalton also did not get the chance to become the part which, with the end of the Cold War, could have been a very good, and certainly more complex, one. If Dalton did not really seem at ease in his role, and never really relaxed into it, which may indeed have been his intention, that ease, however, had become almost complacent and stagy, as well as crowd-pleasing, with Moore. The action scenes in the Dalton films were good, and the settings workable, although the love interests did not really excite and did not appear to engage the somewhat stilted Dalton.

The financial context was problematic. *The Living Daylights*, with $191,200,000, grossed enough to be comparable with the Moore films at their height, but *Licence to Kill*, with $156,200,000, reflected a fall comparable to *A View to a Kill*. Moreover, *The Living Daylights* was only seen by an estimated 14.2 million Americans, the lowest figure since *The Man with the Golden Gun*. Seen by 11.7 million Americans, *Licence to Kill* was affected by competition from *Batman*, *Indiana Jones and the Last Crusade*, and *Lethal Weapon II*, all of which had started before Bond and were having a very good run, which made it difficult to find the screens and audience for the Bond film. *Lethal Weapon II* and *Indiana Jones and the Last Crusade* were also funnier than Bond. It was also too early for the audience to embrace this grittier Bond film.

Again, there was discussion about the long-term viability of the Bond franchise. Costs had led to *Licence to Kill* being shot in Mexico, not Britain. More seriously, there was a bitter legal battle over television distribution rights for Bond films, a case only solved in early 1993. At the same time, the past value of the franchise in the shape of television rights created the need for more products in the shape of new films.

7

THE BROSNAN ERA

If a new Bond presented a change, so, even more, did international developments at this point. The Cold War ended abruptly in 1989 and the Soviet Union imploded in 1991. Earlier, 1991 also saw the United States and Britain at war with Saddam Hussein's Iraq in response to its invasion of Kuwait the previous year. If many of the Bond films had not treated the Cold War as their major theme, less so in practice than other spy films, it had always been there. This was so in *Moonraker* (1979) when there had been cooperation at the close between the United States and the Soviet Union against Drax, and again in *Octopussy* (1983) and *A View to a Kill* (1985) when there had been a measure of cooperation. Now the very context was transformed.

And in many ways. Indeed 2003 proved the nadir of my association with James Bond. The Department of English at the University of Indiana invited me to give the closing plenary lecture at a three-day conference, "The Cultural Politics of Ian Fleming and 007," to mark the fiftieth anniversary of the publication of *Casino Royale*, the first Bond novel. The Lilly Library at Bloomington contains the drafts of the Bond novels because these were added when it bought, from his heirs, Fleming's impressive collection of books (mostly scientific) that first introduced important ideas.

This was a collection he had made, in part to alleviate boredom, in the 1930s when such works were relatively inexpensive. With my mission in sight, I wrote a new paper, on changing images of the United States in the Bond corpus.

I had been given one and a half hours for the talk, instead of the one hour I had anticipated and, as a result, used the opportunity to offer a friendly and helpful review of what we had heard, with particular reference to what needed to be done in order to prepare the papers for publication. Dividing the papers into two categories, I remarked that both were good but required some consideration. For the historical, I argued that chronological specificity was required: it was not generally sufficient to refer to the Cold War and Bond. Instead, it was necessary to make it clear whether 1953, 1955, or 1957, and so on, was at issue. For cultural studies, I suggested that, unless it could be shown that they were crucial to the audience or to many of the plots, I could not see the point of having two essays devoted to lesbian readings of James Bond. I did not have time to deal with the anal-retentive themes offered by one of the speakers.

My mild comments led to me being accused of being homophobic, which I am not, and of trying to close down debate, which was inaccurate. Excluded from the subsequent business meeting to discuss proceedings, I was criticized there. I sent in my paper for publication only to have it ignored. The organizer refused to return my calls. And so on. . . . A brief account, by Andrew Lycett, the Fleming biographer, surfaced in "Lesbians and 007—a licence to deconstruct," prominently published in the *Sunday Times* [of London] on June 8, 2003. Lycett referred to my drawing "fire from the lesbian contingent."

Well, the conference organizers paid what they owed, which had become my main concern, and I published my piece elsewhere. I was, however, attacked in the subsequent conference book, *Ian Fleming and James Bond: The Cultural Politics of 007*, edited by Edward Comentale, Stephen Watt, and Skip Willman (2005), the editors offering a wonderfully weaselly (no, that is unfair to weasels) way of getting around the fact that, in the name of the freedom of intellectual life, which I had supposedly violated by my mild criticisms and suggestions, I had been bulleted from the published proceedings.

The latter incidentally included such cultural studies gems as the following: "This 'arche' is the sense of an aboriginal empowerment, as if the Bond figure carried with it the moment of the commencement of the Law of the Father," "this, in the end, may be why dykes like Bond: because the man who wears gender as a style rather than an essence, effects conversion to his side through better technique, thrives on heat between equals, and provides women the thrill of sex unprotected by heterosexual privacy and respectability, could, in the end, just turn out to be a woman"— this last from "Lesbian Bondage, or Why Dykes Like 007"—and "*Diamonds* is both obsessed by the anal and suffused with a subtle, but insistent panic about masculine identity, which are, of course, ultimately related." One of the pieces misunderstood the attitudes of Fleming by arguing that he presented the SIS as a bureaucratic world akin to SPECTRE, whereas, in practice, he greatly praised it, as in *Moonraker*, and offered a clear depiction of evil to provide a bedrock of value and values.

The issue to me was the extent to which the editors seemed to believe that criticism infringes academic freedom, and that anything otherwise goes as far as papers are concerned. At times, this had a farcical quality in the conference. One speaker, discussing postcolonialism and the film *The Man with the Golden Gun*, claimed that most of it had been set in Hong Kong. When I pointed out that, after an opening scene in Hong Kong, most of the rest of the action was set in Bangkok, he retorted that the canals in question were those in Hong Kong. I said that actually this was inaccurate, that the city was Bangkok, and that Thailand, never occupied by a Western power, was not a country that could be described as postcolonial—only to be told that I was misguided. All academic nonsense, but also a record of the extent to which the supposed cultural significance of Bond was becoming more of an issue as the franchise both continued and prospered. Bond was embedded, not in an army, but in America's "culture wars," a conflict that was self-serving and repetitive, and one where cultural icons provided both topic and weapons.

In practice, the franchise had been continued after Dalton and prospered. There had been much speculation after *Licence to Kill* (1989) that Bond was over, because there was a major gap before the next film, which was *GoldenEye* (1995). The gap meant that Dalton pulled out and was unable to play the transition of Bond into the post–Cold War world. In April 1994, he announced that he would not appear in the follow-up, which was to be *GoldenEye*. Indeed, the original script was written in 1993 with Dalton in mind, a priority that ensured that there was not to be much humor. Ten actors were then tested for the role, but it was offered to Pierce Brosnan who, unlike after Moore, was now free to accept it. Brosnan told the press when he was introduced for the role in June 1994 that he would like "to see what is beneath the surface of this man," but, in practice, he followed the format.

In *GoldenEye*, Brosnan appeared to enjoy the role, although Robbie Coltrane, as the likable Russian gangster Valentin Zukovsky, and Sean Bean, as Valentin's villainous rival, the head of the Janus Syndicate, were more impressive actors. Zukovsky was a version of Boris Yeltsin, albeit nicer, smarter, and not so drunk. In contrast, Bean presented a Putin type. The top Janus killer, Xenia Onatopp, played by Famke Janssen, a murderous ex–fighter pilot who squeezes victims to death with her thighs, attaining orgasm in the process, is a powerful presence in every scene she appears in. She is given suggestive lines, as with her telling Bond that she likes her vodka martini "straight up, vis a tvist."

GoldenEye worked, and worked very well, as an adventure film. From the opening sequence, set in 1986, breaking into a Soviet chemical weapons base after a bungee jump from the top of a very high dam (640 feet), there was a high pitch of adventure with a strong pace. The special effects were ridiculous, notably with Bond's escape from the base, from motorbike to plunging aircraft, but the audience did not mind and, indeed, expected such effects. They also got them, with Bond commandeering a tank and careering around the streets of St. Petersburg, beating pursuing police cars, and with the villain's armored train. Bond uses his tank to derail the advancing train. The tank chase was filmed in St. Petersburg in April 1994. The person responsible for the permission to film the tank chase was at the time an unknown former KGB agent, one Vladimir Putin who, from 1991 to 1996, was the head of the "Committee for External Relations of the Saint Petersburg Mayor's Office, with responsibility for promoting international relations and foreign investments."

The setting, largely in post-Soviet Russia, helped provide a theme of mystery in that the intentions and reasons of the villainy were long unclear, as, more significantly, was the identity of the villain. The revelation that the motivations of Janus, the supposedly dead Alec Trevelyan, the former agent 006 (ably played in both roles by Sean Bean), looked back to Britain handing over Cossacks (including his parents), who had fought for the Germans, to the Soviet Union in 1945, which slaughtered them, provided a more pointed reason than megalomania. Janus, the head of a mysterious and powerful criminal network, was really Trevelyan, and that the latter had been a traitor in MI6 put Britain on a level with Russia; General Ouromov, a traitor in Russian security, also played a major role in the plot.

Indeed, in the film there was a general theme of dissolution and uncertainty that was more pointed than the usual concerns about megalomaniacs. This theme was captured with the discarded statues of the Soviet leaders. These were a motif in the excellent pre-film credits, where the figure of Lenin is smashed, and an impressive setting for the dramatic nighttime first meeting between Bond and Janus. Such statue dumps indeed littered the ex-Communist countries. The idea of two kinds of Russian criminal added a welcome complexity to the plot.

In place of Dalton's introspection, doubt, and angst, Brosnan provided cool sophistication. Opening in the United States on November 17, 1995, and in London five days later, *GoldenEye* started a new financial streak. Adjusted for inflation, it grossed $350.7 million worldwide, compared to $203 million, the previous record, for *Moonraker*. The final American admission figures were 29 million, while the British box office takings were £19.9 million. The reviews were very positive, both in Britain and the United States. The film had delivered to its viewers dramatic episodes and strong characters. John Gardner's novel, based on the screenplay, had Trevelyan intent on causing "a world-wide financial meltdown," with Britain once more entering "the Stone Age." Bond retorts, "All so that mad little Alec can settle a score with the world fifty years on. So you can settle an injustice done to your ancestors," only for Trevelyan to reply, "Spare me any Freudian analysis."

Despite the end of the Cold War in 1989, new villains were readily found for Bond to confront, starting with Trevelyan. Brosnan was far better than Arnold Schwarzenegger in *True Lies* (1994). In the next Bond film, *Tomorrow Never Dies* (1997), the megalomaniac villain, Elliot Carver, played by Jonathan Pryce, was an international media baron, with deliberate echoes of Rupert Murdoch, which were fully recognized at the time. These echoes were seen not least in the attempt by both to win access to the Chinese market, in particular for Carver by increasing the circulation of his newspaper *Tomorrow*, as well as how best to increase his satellite television take. Carver's ambition was presented as that of a psychopath, willing to see his wife killed because she had had a relationship with Bond in the past. Carver cavorted before a screen instructing subordinates to cause chaos around the world. Causing war between Britain and China was part of the villain's equation. Carver declared, "You give me the pictures. I'll give you the war," words attributed to William Randolph Hearst with reference to America's war with Spain in 1898. Subscribers to Carver's television system would be shown the war. In some respects, this was the swan song of conventional media; nowadays, Carver's empire would be on social media, planting lies by means of Twitter.

However, the idea that it was Britain rather than the United States that was China's adversary in nearby waters strained credulity. The scenes of British warships, at the start and end of the film, were redolent of a past age. This theme of the past was readily captured by the employment of a naval gun to sink the villain's stealth warship at the close, rather than the more commonplace use by then of a guided missile. The navy's embrace of new technology had been displayed at the start when a British warship, the fictional HMS *Chester*, launches a cruise missile against a "terrorist arms bazaar on the Russian border," only for the missile to fail to respond when an attempt is made to abort it. The contrast with the use of the gun reflected the "anti-modernist" strand that can at times be found in the Bond films. This was very much seen with the opposition to a reliance on signals intelligence, increasingly the norm for the United States, as opposed to the human element represented by Bond. At the same time, a gun was showier than a missile, while the latter would encounter problems with a stealth target.

The villain in this film, Carver, as in so many other films, is engaged with new technology, notably in altering GPS locations to cause war between Britain and China, and in his stealth warship and the remote-control drill used to sink opposing warships, a drill that does for Carver at the close. More benignly, Bond benefited in Hamburg from a remote-controlled BMW-750, an instance of BMW's product placement.

Aside from Judi Dench as a tougher, more modern M, the female lead had changed dramatically. *Tomorrow Never Dies* provided an effective female action-lead, Chinese agent (of the People's External Security Force) Wai Lin, played by Michelle Yeoh, as Bond's partner—one who could have been a Bond. Indeed, Brosnan called her "his Chinese counterpart," and she was very different to Paris Carver. Yeoh starred in many martial arts Asian cinema films before she joined Bond and her inclusion in the film represented an inclusion of aspects of the genre, including the use of the fighting style. So, also, with *Die Another Day* (2002), in which Halle Berry, in this case the American agent, Jinx, was a highly effective female partner for Bond. Denise Richards as Christmas Jones in *The World Is Not Enough* was an unlikely nuclear physicist, but that was the role she received. It also permitted Bond's line: "I've always wanted to have Christmas in Turkey." The color indicator noted by Umberto Eco in 1965, with the darker woman as more likely to be villainous, was put aside, notably with the presentation of the Miranda Frost character in *Die Another Day*: a blond, Harvard-educated MI6 agent, she turned out to be a baddie, unlike the Halle Berry character.

The Bond character meanwhile changed. Smoking and, to a lesser extent, gambling became less prominent and Bond only had a drink rarely. In *Tomorrow Never Dies*, Bond, at the outset, refers to smoking as a "filthy habit," while knocking out a smoking thug. Ironically, it was still acceptable to have an agent who blew up and shot large numbers of people, but then that was not discretionary for an adventure hero even though such conduct scarcely conformed to that of British secret agents. Indeed, MI6 made much of not killing. In addition, whereas adventure films in the 1950s had not seen such carnage unless they involved science fiction, by the 1990s norms were very different.

Aside from the move away from smoking and drinking, Bond, moreover, was now a serial monogamist and sex played little role in the characterization, although still more than was to be the case with the portrayal by Daniel Craig. In the Bond-like *True Lies* (1994), Arnold Schwarzenegger played a secret agent with a wife and daughter.

Style had clearly changed, not least as it had been democratized. In *Licence to Kill* (1989), Sanchez tells Bond, "You have class," but there was no longer a secure basis for the representation of class, either in Britain or in the United States. Whereas the trailer for *From Russia, With Love* (1963) referred to Bond as the "toughest, wiliest gentleman agent," the trailer for the collected video edition of 1996 called him the "original action hero." The stylish, gentlemanly conduct of the original Bond could now seem effete, certainly as compared to portrayals by Bruce Willis, the blue-collar anti-Bond in many respects. Instead, the Bond films now offered a different, updated account of style. There was no role for complicated discussions of how best to cheat and win at bridge, and no careful listing of the details of meals, although they had been characteristic of the novels. Indeed, the problematic representation of class was seen in the repeated ironies of the Bond character on the screen.

Moreover, Bond's search for megalomaniac billionaires in exotic locales had become stale and formulaic. In one respect, the character, whether played by Moore or by Brosnan, was distanced from any serious discussion of role or mission. In part, this reflected the nature of film and, specifically, the change to a more hectic and chaotic editing and lack of "slow" passages to retain the interest of those with attention deficit. The related "dumbing down" of culture described by many commentators also played a role.

At the same time, the role was probed, and notably in *Golden-Eye*, with both Trevelyan and the lead female character, Natalya Simonova, a "goody" played by Izabella Scorupco, doubting Bond, as in a way did M, who calls him "a sexist, misogynist dinosaur." More immediately, Trevelyan responds to Bond's criticisms: "I might as well ask you if all the vodka martinis ever silence the screams of all the men you've killed, or if you find forgiveness in the arms of all those willing women for the dead ones you failed to protect." Simonova was right-on: "You think I'm impressed? All of you with your guns, your killing, your death?" Simonova was wrong; there was a clear difference between the two sides, but to most viewers, virtue partly seemed to come from the barrel of a gun. This was a perversion of the character as invented by Fleming, but that was not a context that meant anything.

In *Tomorrow Never Dies*, there was a degree of humor, especially with the psychotic doctor, but not the weak parody seen in the later Moore films. Brosnan was more convincingly dangerous as well as athletic than Moore. There was also the pathos of the death of a former lover, Carver's wife, Paris, murdered because Bond had revived their relationship. However, the film became increasingly violent and a matter of one chase or fight after another.

The World Is Not Enough (1999) offered villainy separated into two individuals, and a degree of plot complexity accordingly. The high-speed boat chase in London along the River Thames was a particularly exciting section near the opening. It followed an attack on a now-vulnerable MI6 building. The plot involved a threat to the supply of oil to the West, more developed than in *Never Say Never Again* (1983). Villainy was split between two characters, each of whom was very disturbing in psychological terms. Indeed, Electra King emerges as a sadist, while Renard, a former KGB assassin thrown out for mental reasons and turned high-tech terrorist for hire, cannot feel pain. After Janus in *GoldenEye*, he was another former agent who used his skills for his personal gain, again an aspect of the supposed "End of History" or at least ideology.

The collapse of the Soviet Union provided a key context for this film, notably with the future of nuclear weaponry. The former Soviet Union as a sphere for chaos was also seen in the "James Bond in miniature" offered by Anthony Horowitz in his "Alex Rider" adventure *Ark Angel* (2005), the sixth of his series. America did not feature in *The World Is Not Enough*. Instead, Britain is the key player and the geopolitics are those of oil. The key is production in Azerbaijan and a British-backed plan by the King family to build a pipeline from there to the Mediterranean, bypassing Russian-controlled pipelines and areas. This is a different remedy to *The Man with the Golden Gun*, but one both more based in reality and drawing on British geopolitical ideas at the close of World War I. In turn, the villains seek to profit further, aiming to destroy the alternative routes from the Black Sea by blowing up in the Bosporus an ex-Soviet nuclear submarine containing nuclear fission material stolen from Kazakhstan. Renard has turned Electra, his former prisoner, so that she cooperates in this deadly plan. *The World Is Not Enough* took $362 million worldwide, of which a third was in the United States.

In contrast to the earlier Brosnan Bond films, the North Korean villainy in *Die Another Day* was unconvincing, not least in a confused and highly confusing plot of globalization, genetic manipulation, and North Korean expansionism. The settings were varied, including Cuba, London, Iceland, and North Korea. This helped ensure the variety of pace seen in the film, a variety assisted by the focus on new technology, notably cars but also gene therapy, which was explained at some length. The invisible car that Bond used, an Aston Martin V12 Vanquish designed for extreme cold and equipped with twin missile launchers, a jet engine booster, a self-destruct mechanism, and a laser beam–type slasher, was his principal non-human assistant, but other assets included a ring that can emit a sound shattering bulletproof glass and a surfboard containing a hidden compartment that holds a gun, plastic explosives, and a detonator. There were also references to previous films, providing a ready way to establish continuity. Halle Berry appearing from the sea with a knife at her waist was an echo of Ursula Andress's entrance in *Dr. No*. Moreover, visiting Q's laboratory, Bond picks up Rosa Klebb's flick-knife-armed shoe from *From Russia, With Love* and sees "Little Nellie" from *You Only Live Twice*.

By 2002, however, the forty-nine-year-old Brosnan appeared tired and some of the scenes were particularly ridiculous, notably the surfing escape from Iceland. The theme song was terrible. Some of the reviews were very critical. In the *Times*, Barbara Ellen described the plot as "more worn than a pair of old keks and a script more wooden than a ski lodge . . . high-tech gadgetry marvels that only strange middle-aged men who still live with their mothers could get excited about . . . explosions of overacting."

Appearing in 2002, with the first sequences shot in December 2001, this was a film that appeared more seriously dated in the aftermath of the September 2001 terrorist attacks on New York and Washington. These attacks opened a need for new plots. At the same time, the profitability of the franchise was clear. *Die Another Day* broke all records to become the top-taking Bond film with $432 million worldwide, a third of which was in the United States.

8

THE AGE OF CRAIG

Blunt and to the point, Daniel Craig made it abundantly clear that he had not liked playing Bond, whom he referred to as a sexist, misogynist dinosaur. Nevertheless, Craig certainly rebooted the Bond franchise. In particular, Craig adapted Bond to make it possible to meet the challenge posed, from 2002, by the Jason Bourne films. In doing so, Craig helped Bond to retain market appeal and, even more, to reach out to a new, younger audience, greatly influenced by the film styles of pop videos, of video action, and of the Hong Kong style of martial arts action films.

Bourne was based on a series of novels by the prolific American adventure writer Robert Ludlum. *The Bourne Identity* (2002) saw Matt Damon create a wronged amnesiac government assassin in a film with great drive—drive aided by an impressive jumpy camerawork style. He returned in three sequels, although not in the muddled *Bourne Legacy* (2012). In the second and third films, *The Bourne Supremacy* (2004) and then *The Bourne Ultimatum* (2007), a new director, Paul Greengrass, offered a hectic style. The most recent in the sequence, *Jason Bourne* (2016), also directed by Greengrass, saw Bourne very much in the here and now, with references to a billionaire social media tycoon permitting government-sponsored data hacking. London was one of the settings, and there was a very impressive scene in Athens, but this was a series about the United States: Bourne was the hero and the CIA the villain.

Born in 1953, Pierce Brosnan had appeared tired and stilted by his last Bond performance. In contrast, Craig in his first Bond film, *Casino Royale* (2006), offered a more hard-edged approach. Like Connery, but not Moore, Craig captured the grittiness, hard edge, and brutal violence of Bond that Fleming intended. The early scene of Craig killing a villain in a toilet (which Americans hilariously describe as a restroom), holding down his head to drown him in a sink after a bitter and fully displayed fight, captured a sense of menace that had been lacking since Connery. Moreover, this fight, like other Craig action scenes, was, in practice, more violent than the killings allowed to Connery. Bond went on to execute a defenseless British traitor, and thus gain his 00 status, in a scene that had similarities to the killing of the villainous geologist in *Dr. No*. Craig delivered a convincing determination as a killer even as he was also shown as emotionally vulnerable.

There were too many action scenes in *Casino Royale*, excessive violence, and a jumbled and overly long and sprawling plot, but there was much else. The poker sequence in the casino was convincing, as was the torture scene. Moreover, there was room for romance with Vesper Lynd. Poker replaced baccarat. Poker was much more popular, so there was no need to explain the rules to the audience, which would have been necessary if the gamblers had played baccarat. The film set a record for box office receipts, taking $594 million (£374.5 million) worldwide. Over a quarter of the takings were in the United States, ensuring that with that film, the franchise had generated $1.4 billion there. At the same time this percentage was less than that for the Brosnan films, which underlined the global nature of the product. British box office takings were £55.6 million, a considerable increase on the Brosnan films, for which the record had been £36.1 million for *Die Another Day*.

The year 2008, in contrast, was a mixed year for Bond. He had been cast as a limp, dated marionette in a misconceived novel by Sebastian Faulks (*Devil May Care*, 2008), and the hundredth anniversary of his creator's birth had been the occasion for some strikingly unoriginal media coverage, not least a weak radio documentary. To cap it all, the film that year, *The Quantum of Solace*, was not treated kindly by reviewers. They said it required too great an understanding of the previous venture, *Casino Royale*, which was indeed a coda to it, and were cool to the new film. *Quantum of Solace* of course had its flaws, in particular the lackluster credits and the theme song. Indeed, can anyone remember the lyrics of the latter? Yet, the film as a whole worked, and worked well. The criticism of needing to know the previous film well was unwarranted; the dead Vesper was more a plot device that provided a cause for the action, a cause that drives Bond, than an issue throughout the film. The new film started its story immediately after the other closed, with far more continuity than in the films in which Blofeld appeared, and this continuity worked.

The puzzle, in the new film, was the nature and goals of the malign organization, "Quantum," that Bond uncovers. Here the plot was reasonably coherent, with a "baddy" who was more convincing than that in *Casino Royale*, and a challenge that was not that of the by-then-predictable seconds-to-human-destruction type—a type of destruction now mostly left to the "superhero" films. The account of sinister Bolivian generals linked to an international conspiracy hiding behind the cover of environmentalism worked reasonably well, even if it scarcely frightened, which disappointed some viewers. Control over water supplies was certainly modish as an issue, but it was also convincing. There are fewer disjointed chases and less fighting than in *Casino Royale*, but the special effects were good, as was the very stylish sequence set in the lakeside opera, both on and off stage. The fighting was brutal. Unusually, 007, mourning for Vesper, did not seduce the female lead.

There was the repeated criticism that Craig was not Connery, that specifically his Bond was not a figure of wit. Indeed, there were very few quips in *Quantum*. However, just as Faulks got it wrong by taking Bond back into the 1960s, so critics needed to consider that it is not terribly helpful to judge the Bond of the 2000s as if he should be in a 1960s film. There was a little too much Bourne in the Craig films, and their quota of action was too high, but that reflected the global audience. Within these constraints, *Quantum* was highly successful.

Financially, the franchise got better. Sam Mendes, a major director, helped give an edge to *Skyfall* (2012), which marked the fiftieth anniversary of the first of the films, *Dr. No*, and earned $1 billion at the box office, putting it ahead of the earlier films, even adjusting for inflation. The plot, at once complex psychologically and all too simple in practice, had serious flaws, with the villain, Silva, played by Javier Bardem, taking vengefulness to the point of insanity. The villain's background and cause represented a struggle within the service for only the second time: *GoldenEye* was the other. M had handed Silva over to the Chinese when they were about to capture him anyway and, in return, received six already-captured agents. Questioned under torture by the Chinese for months, Silva demands that M should "Think on your sins," adding the need for her to confront the consequences of his having taken a cyanide pill: "Look upon your work, Mother."

The vengeful Silva attacks the headquarters of MI6, although this has less shock value than the first such attack in a Bond film, in *The World Is Not Enough*. Both attacks revealed that villains could also show technological proficiency, a continued theme in the series and one that reflected its anti-modernist character. In *Skyfall*, the talented and dangerously knowledgeable Silva is able to penetrate electronically the environmental system used by MI6, in order to break down the safety protocols and turn on the gas. This leads to an explosion that destroys M's office and kills several MI6 officers, thus revealing British vulnerability at the most central point. This dramatic and very public failure results in governmental criticism. M complains that MI6 is being treated as "a bunch of antiquated bloody idiots fighting a war we don't understand and can't possibly win." In practice, this remark offers a link both to a sense of Britain as under threat, but also to the need to keep the Bond corpus fit for purpose.

Bond is certainly under challenge, and not only because he must drink Heineken beer, not shaken martinis, due to Heineken's sponsorship of the film. At the start, he fails to defeat the villain. Patrice, an assassin in Silva's employ, has in Istanbul seized the hard drive containing the true identities of NATO agents located undercover in terrorist organizations. In a fabulous chase, Bond tries hard, but Patrice thwarts him. Indeed, Bond, fighting Patrice on top of a train, is accidentally shot by Moneypenny, another agent, who is aiming at Patrice. Badly wounded, Bond nearly drowns when he falls to the river deep below. The shot has been taken at the repeated order of M, who is shown as resolute but unable to control the situation effectively from a distance.

Bond disappears and loses interest in the Service. This is a rebellion that is very different in kind to that of Silva, but that, similarly, reflects the role of individual responses. Bond drops out and, indeed, is believed dead by MI6. He only returns after Silva's attack on MI6's headquarters and, when he does so, is an apparent wreck. Far from ready for action, Bond has a graying beard and eyes that are red from alcoholism.

As a result, Bond, as in the novel *The Man with the Golden Gun* (1965), has to be brought back into the Service. In the film, this involves physical and psychological tests—tests that he cannot master. Mallory, the Chair of the Intelligence and Security Committee (ably played by Ralph Fiennes), urges Bond to face realities: "It's a young man's game. Look, you've been seriously injured, there's no shame in saying you've lost a step. The only shame would be in not admitting it until it's too late." In the repeated pattern of the villain mocking Bond, Silva takes forward this sense of Bond's aging and failure: "All the physical stuff—so dull, so dull. Chasing spies—so old-fashioned. Your knees must be killing you. England, the Empire, MI6. You're living in a ruin as well; you just don't know it yet."

Pushing M to the fore in the film was an aspect of Bond as a "buddy movie," albeit a buddy with a maternal, caring aspect, indeed a mother-son film. She stands by Bond despite his test scores and his recent history. The buddy now was M, not Leiter, and, although this relationship was organizationally silly, it worked emotionally. M herself appears redundant because of Silva's initial successes. She is asked to retire after the hard drive is stolen. M, however, is determined to fight on. At the same time, Silva tests her purpose by calling forth her past treatment of him.

Silva's hatred drives him to mount another attack on the center of British authority, in this case a parliamentary hearing, indeed a hearing on MI6, which thus brings the plot together. Mallory, however, proves equal to the challenge. He responds to Silva's attack, as M is unable and even unwilling to do, joining Bond in fighting back; although Mallory himself has already been wounded. His backstory provides an image of decisiveness that belies his bureaucratic identity at that moment. He has been a Lieutenant Colonel in the army and had been captured by the IRA and survived. He is fit, ready to kill, and able to take pain.

Silva, in turn, is a new stage in the deadly terrorism Britain must face.

Bond, moreover, recovers. Although still injured, he is able to attack Patrice and beat him. Bond also is able to respond to a now very young Q, who treats him as an anachronism. They first meet in another central place of British identity, the National Gallery in London. Moreover, a totemic item is selected as the backdrop: J. M. W. Turner's painting *The Fighting Temeraire towed to her last berth to be broken up* (1839). This painting, which has been polled as the most popular with the British public, is a visual account of the end of the age of Fighting Sail, and shows a mighty ship-of-the-line that is now redundant in the age of steam and is being towed by a steam-powered tug. Q makes his point clear: "It always makes me feel a little melancholy. The grand old warship being ignominiously hauled away for scrap. . . . The inevitability of time, don't you think?" Bond has a different response. What he sees is "a very big ship." Ironically, although the *Temeraire* was, in 1839, a ship from a past age, in the nineteenth century Britain was to dominate the new age, that of steam-powered warships.

Q and Bond continue. Q claims that "Age is no guarantee of efficiency," only for Bond to reply, "And youth is no guarantee of innovation." To a certain extent, this is a reprise of a theme repeatedly seen in the Bond corpus, that of the competition between expertise in technology and that of the agent in the field: the belief in the value of digital information, for example, as manipulated by Janus's assistant Boris Grishenko in *GoldenEye*, against the analog human information. Ultimately, in *Skyfall*, Bond and Q cooperate, and, as so often in the films, this helps ensure success, in this case against Silva. The two men combine to break Silva's code, with Q able to understand how it works, but Bond identifying the keyword, in part because of the experience of his age.

The death of M, bleeding to death after being shot by one of Silva's men, proved a cathartic close to the film, rather like that of Vesper Lynd in *Casino Royale*, but one that worked better. This was the first death of an M in a Bond story. On the other hand, the lengthy final shootout in Scotland, with its echoes of the villains attacking an isolated farm in a Western, could seem formulaic. It was certainly long. Nevertheless, there was a psychological reason. Bond must return to Skyfall, his family's Scottish home, a remote building in a difficult landscape, in order to confront his issues, notably over his parents' death. This is certainly a back-to-the-past theme, but that is a standard theme of heroic tales, and notably those of the epic character.

In this shootout, Bond uses the Aston Martin from *Goldfinger* in another echo of the past—an echo that offers a use of firepower to counter Silva's superiority at that stage in manpower and firepower. This is also the revenge of the past: as with the use of a naval gun, rather than missiles, by the Royal Navy at the close of *Tomorrow Never Dies*, so in *Skyfall* the old family retainer places a hunting knife on the table with "sometimes the old ways are the best." M and Bond rely on simple devices to destroy one of Silva's helicopters. In the fight-out, the house Skyfall is destroyed, but, with his knowledge of the location, Bond escapes through a tunnel under the house, before he kills his opponents. With the death of M, in effect his foster mother, Bond is finally able to leave the past and face the future.

At the close of the film, Bond returns to London. Mallory is now M, in an office very like that of M's in *Dr. No*, while a new Moneypenny is in place, the agent who accidentally shot him in Turkey in the struggle with Patrice which, in a way, reboots this relationship. Bond himself is ready to return to his missions, his angst, as in the novel *Casino Royale*, a feature of the past. The film indeed offers key images of Britishness near the end, not only the Big Ben that had featured in the first film, *Dr. No*, but also the Houses of Parliament and the British flag. The launch of *Skyfall* saw a major feast of Bond popular culture, including "Designing 007: 50 Years of Bond Style," a major show in London. This was appropriate; much of *Skyfall* involved very deliberate echoes of earlier films.

Spectre (2015) also proved extraordinarily successful, although it lacked the dramatic focus of *Skyfall* and was not so successful with the critics. There were many deliberate echoes of earlier films, a lengthy but gripping start in Mexico City, a good villain, the effective and interesting new M, a vivid and lengthy nighttime sequence in Rome, a dramatic chase sequence in Switzerland, and a use of familiar London settings. The frequent references in the film to previous Bond films, for example, the fight on the train referring to *From Russia, With Love*, helped provide a knowing character to the films, as well as a sense of linkage. How far this method attracted new viewers is unclear. So also with Bond's personal childhood link with the villain and the highly troubled psychology of the latter. The Austrian Hannes Oberhauser is revealed as Bond's foster father, with Hannes's jealous son, Franz, being Blofeld, the villain. The film also included a discursive section in Morocco that added little, and that did not have the pace of *Jason Bourne* (2016). Bond's ability to kill many, many, villains in that section when he breaks out from the villain's base was scarcely credible.

The survival of the villain offered the prospect of another level of continuity with new films, and followed the trend to serialize the stories of films to a certain extent. Responses to *Spectre* varied, and continue to vary. In September 2016, Fiennes, the new actor playing M, told the *Daily Telegraph* that Russian viewers had complained that *Spectre* was too grave and insufficiently jokey and showy. Also that September, rumors circulated that Craig had been offered £150 million to do two more Bond films.

9

TOWARD A BOND WORLD

The opening sequence of the 2012 London Olympics said it all. In a short film seen by most of the British people, but also by a large chunk of the world's population, Bond goes to Buckingham Palace and meets the Queen; they stroll down a corridor, get into a helicopter, and fly to the Olympic stadium, with the statue of Churchill outside Parliament waving approval. Both Daniel Craig and the Queen apparently parachute in, which was not in fact what happened. National icons combined, with Craig ably playing Bond and some humor provided by the royal corgis (dogs) that seek to accompany the Queen. It was not necessary for a commentator to explain anything, which is a sign of the merger of reality with fiction.

Fleming was far from alone in popular fiction, although nobody broke as successfully into film as he did, even if Tolkien and Rowling came close. Comparisons with other writers in the same genre are instructive. There was a whole raft of writers who had really served as spies, including Somerset Maugham, Graham Greene, David Cornwell (writing as John le Carré), Phil Atkey, Francis Warwick, and Ted Allbeury. The last, in fact, Theodore Edward le Bouthillier Allbeury (1917–2005), offers the most interesting comparison with Fleming, not least with their fathers killed in World War I. Like the latter, notably in his short stories, Allbeury could provide depth of characterization and humanity in his writing, and could handle the details of hardware, technology, and plots. Also like Fleming, Allbeury had an exciting personal life, although, while Fleming was not given to multiple marriages, Allbeury was an enthusiast, having three wives and a number of chaotic adventures. Allbeury certainly did not have Fleming's advantages. He went to a grammar school, not Eton, worked in a foundry and became a tool designer, only to be recruited into army intelligence, having taught himself French and German. Postwar, Allbeury went into advertising, chicken farming, breeding Alsatian dogs, pirate radio, and failing to be elected to Parliament, turning to novels from 1973 to help him get over the carrying off of his four-year-old daughter, Kerry, by her angry mother. Allbeury's *A Choice of Enemies* (1973) was set in the Cold War and saw the hero, Bailey, an ex-spy, forced back into the service. This was followed by a string of rapidly written novels: *The Special Collection* (1975), about the KGB backing trade union chaos in Britain; *The Only Good German* (1976), about the resurgence of Nazism in Germany; *The Man with the President's Mind* (1977), about a Soviet attempt to substitute a changeling; *The Alpha List* (1979), in which the hero has to investigate his closest friend; *The Other Side of Silence* (1981), a fictional version of the Philby case; *All Our Tomorrows* (1982), about a Soviet takeover of Britain; *Pay Any Price* (1983); and *A Wilderness of Mirrors* (1988). Why Fleming, not Allbeury, who wrote well and created well-anchored and suspenseful plots? Probably Fleming's ability to create a character who could be turned into an Anglo-American star was crucial. Allbeury and the others could not manage that, although with the right producer and creative team they could have become quite successful.

The Bond novels and films illustrate the culture and politics of the times and vice versa, although it is the films, indeed, that dominate modern attention, and certainly not the novels. Since the mid-1990s, it has been claimed that over a quarter, or even more, of the world's population has seen a Bond film, ensuring that billions of people have viewed an image of global struggle through Western eyes and the perspective offered by this franchise. Individual films have not done as well as, say, *Star Wars*, but the series as a whole has been more profitable than any other. Comparison with the *Star Wars* series is instructive; while the Bond stories share the interest in technology, they are more adult in every respect. At the same time, the popularity of both reflects the general desire to see life in a moral light and the role this leaves to belief in heroes and their adventures.

More mundanely, references to Bond are frequent throughout modern culture and life. For example, on the BBC radio comedy news program *The News Quiz* on October 15, 2016, the issue of a price war between the British supermarket chain Tesco and its international supplier Unilever was discussed with the description of Unilever as "a strange, commercial version of SPECTRE." In practice, there was no valid comparison between the two, but the use of the reference served to dramatize what was otherwise a somewhat mundane discussion. It is so also with other film and television series such as *Star Trek*, with its "beam me up," "warp speed," and other phrases.

Aside from comforting British viewers about their state's continued role and competence, and lacking any of the doubts expressed, for example, in Fleming's novels and, even more clearly, the novels and films of Len Deighton and John Le Carré, the Bond series also charted shifts in the wider world. However improbable the plot, the films, to work as adventure stories and to provide a background to the fighting, had to be able to resonate with the interests and concerns of viewers. This they did, and themes and developments such as the space race, the energy crisis, nuclear confrontation, microchips, drugs, and environmental degradation were all played out.

Shifts in the Cold War were also noted in the films. In *Moonraker* (1979), the Americans check with the Soviets when their radar shows the space station from which Drax is planning to fire germ-laden globes at the Earth, to confirm that it is not a Soviet space vehicle. In *For Your Eyes Only* (1981), there is a reference to détente. In *The Spy Who Loved Me* (1977), Bond is able to work with the Soviets; in *Octopussy* (1983), there are good and bad Soviets; in *A View to a Kill* (1985), the villain Zorin has totally escaped KGB control, while, in *The Living Daylights* (1987), the KGB head, General Leonid Pushkin, emerges in a positive light, as does the Afghan resistance—the villains being a KGB general and his American partner who plays at being a military commander.

The list of plot options should be extended to include script versions that were discarded. So also with other intended treatments. In 1976, the producer Kevin McClory, the novelist Len Deighton (the author of *The Ipcress File*), and Connery produced a screenplay for a film, *James Bond of the Secret Service*, that was announced as a project later that year, with the screenplay later called *Warhead*. This was to see Blofeld pursuing Operation Hammerhead, a drive for world domination powered by the blackmail offered by seized nuclear devices carried by mechanical sharks, intended to threaten New York and then the Antarctic ice cap. Linked to this, there was to be the assassination of politicians responsible for the pollution of the seas. The determination of United Artists to stop this scotched the project; litigation made it unattractive to Jack Schwartsman, the independent producer. Instead, he bought McClory's rights for a new version of *Thunderball*, thus launching *Never Say Never Again*. Such projects show how Bond could serve many purposes. There are also some very good video games, notably that of *GoldenEye*. Moreover, Bond novels have translated well to audiotapes.

The wider search for political meanings and echoes in the films need not detract from an appreciation of the adventure or the special effects, the chases, the settings, the women, etc., but there are serious problems for the future. If he remains British, Bond might appear an anachronism. As Blofeld had already mocked in *Diamonds Are Forever* (1971), "Surely you haven't come to negotiate, Mr. Bond. Your pitiful little island hasn't even been threatened." Nevertheless, this Britishness is not only part of the frame of reference that ensures continuity for the films. In practice, it is Bond. It is readily possible to discuss the possibility of a black Bond or, less plausibly, a female one, but a Bond who does not work for Britain does not appear credible. Brexit helps deal with the issue of whether a future Bond would be obliged to work for the European Union.

If Britishness, and the desire to resonate with the American market, seen, for example, in making North Korea the source of the villainy in *Die Another Day* (2002), provide the geopolitical axis of the Bond films, displacing the Britain-Empire axis of the novels, there is, in both, a common tendency to treat the rest of the world as a lesser sphere. This sphere is vulnerable to the activities of villains and therefore requires the intervention of Bond and his British and American allies. Thus, in the film *Thunderball* (1965), SPECTRE is based in Paris under philanthropic cover, and SPECTRE No. 2, Largo, is shown being able to park illegally outside the organization and, once recognized, being saluted by a police officer. Similarly, in *You Only Live Twice*, both novel and film (1967), Bond is needed to defeat Blofeld in Japan: the Japanese cannot achieve the task, and, in the novel, cannot even contribute significant assistance, although they very much do so in the full-scale assault on Blofeld's well-defended base, which forms the dramatic and lengthy culmination of the film.

In Western Europe, intelligence services play no major role in the films. Thus, in the pre-credits adventure in *Thunderball*, Bond is assisted by Mademoiselle La Porte, a female agent from the French section of MI6, in killing SPECTRE No. 6; unlike in the novel *Casino Royale*, the French Deuxième Bureau is nowhere to be seen. Similarly, in Italy, Greece, Spain, and Germany, national intelligence services are absent. In *Moonraker*, there is a partly comic fight-out on the Venetian canals without any role for Italy's many police forces. In *Tomorrow Never Dies*, the German BND provide no help for Bond. Geopolitically, there is a vacuum contested between Britain, sometimes with American support, and either SPECTRE or the Soviets, or dangerous megalomaniacs such as Stromberg.

With the novels and the films, the stories drift from Europe. Although Fleming wrote a homage to the distinctive Levantine espionage of Eric Ambler in his novel *From Russia, With Love* (1957), the world of Royale and Piz Gloria was overshadowed by that of Nassau or Las Vegas, and even more so on film. Royale and Piz Gloria were not cities. Fleming's hostile comments on Paris in "A View to a Kill," a short story published in 1960 as part of *For Your Eyes Only* (1960), indicated that the Continent was a somewhat alien sphere that he did not understand or sympathize with. There was no full-length novel set in Germany, despite it being the enemy in World War II.

With the novels and short stories, the British empire provided the authority in the setting outside Europe of North America. This is not so in the films, however, where Africa plays only a minor part—Egypt, significantly, in the film *The Spy Who Loved Me* (1977), and North Africa, less so, in the latter part of *Never Say Never Again* (1983), *The Living Daylights* (1987), and *Casino Royale* (2006)—but again the local governments do not exist. Instead, as with Egypt, the emphasis is on nomadic figures who conjure up *Beau Geste*. Nor does the government of Brazil, in the film *Moonraker* (1979), or of Thailand, in the film *The Man with the Golden Gun* (1974), or of India, in *Octopussy* (1983), play a role.

Non-alignment in the Third World therefore means nonexistence for the local government. It is as if these countries are ungoverned, ripe for exploitation by international megalomaniacs, and waiting for the order (and purposeful glamour) brought by Western intervention in the shape of Bond. Furthermore, the books and films have imperial attitudes to the non-Western world, with the local population primarily presented in terms of native color, for example, in crowded street scenes and festivals, as in the films *Thunderball, Live and Let Die, The Man with the Golden Gun, The Spy Who Loved Me, Never Say Never Again, Octopussy,* and *Spectre*. Mexico appears as primitive as well as exotic and lively in the opening crowd scene in *Spectre*, the ceremonies of religion serving a role not too different from that in *Live and Let Die*. Thus, complexity is ignored.

This is a world away from the ambiguities seen, for example, in the spy novels of Ambler, Deighton, and Le Carré, but the world of Bond is not characterized by ambiguity, either in setting or in ambience. Instead, there is good (including good rogues such as Draco, the head of the Union Corse, in the novel and film *On Her Majesty's Secret Service*), and, more grippingly, bad. It is only in recent films that ambiguity has been offered, and the moral space of the film restructured, with traitors in the secret service, first with Alec Trevelyan, 006, in the film *GoldenEye* (1995). In *Die Another Day* (2002), there is another such traitor, Miranda Frost, who added this new twist to the bad girl–good girl tension seen so often with the earlier Bond; as well as varying the ethnic/color space, Miranda, the bad girl, is, unusually, the blonde. In *Skyfall*, there is the potent legacy of a past traitor—a legacy that is continuing as the traitor has survived.

In the films from *GoldenEye* on to *Skyfall*, the relationship
between Bond and Judi Dench's M, and again with a new M in
Spectre, is far edgier than that with Bernard Lee's earlier and
fatherly M. Thus, the intelligence world is shown as becoming
more troubled and troubling. *GoldenEye* linked themes traditional to the series, not least megalomania and rogue space vessels,
and offered a new site for much of the action—post-Communist
Russia; but the problematic portrayal of the Secret Service is both
novel and striking. Trevelyan asks Bond, "Did you ever ask why?
Why we toppled all these dictators?" and Bond's answer, that it
was their job to do so, is mocked.

In another note of novelty, *Tomorrow Never Dies* (1997)
shows interdepartmental rivalry at the outset, as the British Minister of Defence takes contrary advice on whether to fire a cruise
missile, with Roebuck, the stiff, arrogant British admiral, accusing
Judi Dench's M of having no balls, only to receive the apt rejoin-
der that at least she does not think with them. M warns that there
might be atomic weaponry in the arms bazaar, Roebuck presses
for action, the minister backs him, only for M's caution to be
vindicated. Bond saves the day, the human element more relevant than the missile, but then he must; the military's control over
its rockets has also failed.

The cultural role can be taken further by contrasting Bond
with spoofs, such as the epicene James Bind, a ludicrous oppo-
nent of STENCH (the Society for the Total Extermination of
Non-Conforming Humans), in *Carry on Spying* (1964); Mike
Myers in *Austin Powers: International Man of Mystery* (1997); or
Rowan Atkinson as *Johnny English* (2003). There are also other
agents who in some way seek to emulate Bond, such as Arnold
Schwarzenegger in *True Lies*, or very obviously differ, notably
Michael Caine's Harry Palmer in the films of the more ambiva-
lent Len Deighton stories, and Matt Damon as Jason Bourne.

The emphasis on the role of the individual in the Bond novels and films is a clear opportunity to provide the last-minute cliff-hanger, but also to comment on a cultural clash that helps to structure the works and the world. The villains believe in planning, almost obsessively so, and, indeed, represent a conflation of plutocratic and bureaucratic man, the last understood by Fleming as a characteristic of Communism. In Weberian terms, Bond is, not represents, but is, the persistence of charisma against the iron cage of rationalism and bureaucracy. Planning is necessary, not only for the villains' complex schemes, but also because they are control freaks, seeking order even as they pursue disorder. In the films, Stromberg and Drax are unhinged utopian planners. In *The Spy Who Loved Me* (1977), Stromberg claims that modern civilization is corrupt and decadent, that it would inevitably destroy itself, and that he is merely accelerating the process when he plans a nuclear holocaust followed by the construction of a new civilization under the sea. In the film *Moonraker* (1979), Drax has similar hopes for a perfect space-based civilization that will link eugenics and technology. These themes are now employed in the comic films, including those with Marvel characters.

In *GoldenEye* (1995), Bond is up against not only M's reliance on statistical analysis ("the evil Queen of Numbers," in the words of the Chief of Staff, Bill Tanner, is wrongly convinced that the Russians cannot have a GoldenEye project), but also against Trevelyan's belief in planning, almost an obsession with it. Aside from the meticulous planning of his project, Trevelyan tells Bond when he breaks into his armored train, "Situation analysis hopeless. You have no backup." When Bond triumphs in that film, it is an individualism ("Bond. Only Bond," as Trevelyan remarks) of selfless dedication and loyalty that wins, not the selfishness of Trevelyan and his confidence in systems analysis and planning. This is similar to the contrast in Fleming's novel *Moonraker* (1955) between Bond and Drax.

In practice, individualism was, for some critics, somewhat compromised in the films by the repeated efforts at product placement. Whereas Bond was in part created by these means in the novels, the placement there intended more to suggest individual distinction and quality than to encourage sales, the situation was somewhat different in the films, especially with the cars. The distinction, however, is still given Bond in his outfits and language, as in the film *Moonraker* when, having damaged his clothes escaping from the cable car in Rio de Janeiro, he is asked if he has broken something: "Only my tailor's heart." Product placement represents an embrace of international capitalism very different from the view of it provided by Fleming's depiction of SPECTRE in the novel *Thunderball*. Instead, there it is the range of trade links that is notable. For example, Mafia heroin, captured in Naples, had been sold in Los Angeles.

Product placement for the Bond stories is an aspect of readily grasped opulence and internationalism, notably with the cars. Thus, when Junius Du Pont entertains Bond in *Goldfinger*, Fleming has him order two pints of pink champagne. "The Pommery '50. Silver tankards," with two double vodka martinis each to start. Read on, though. Having had the best meal he had ever had as a sequel—stone crabs, about which Fleming is knowledgeable, as he would have been, Bond is suddenly "revolted. . . . It was the puritan in him that couldn't take it." Fleming probes that conundrum: opulence is to be enjoyed, but not at the expense of the mission.

Popular culture is readier to work with apparent meanings that are accessible and attractive, rather than to pursue implausible and self-referential academic approaches and interests and their criticisms. Because these apparent meanings are very much up to date in their political concerns, the stylish Bond works as a defender of the West in the here and now. Indeed, the question of the future of Bond frequently rests for popular audiences on the issue of where the villainy will come from. Thus, from 2001, there was the issue of whether, and, if so, how, the Bond corpus would relate to the threat from bin Laden and his successors. This threat, indeed, created problems in terms of market response and credibility. Any depiction of Muslims or, solely, Arabs must avoid the suggestion that more than a minority are villains, but this is a difficult task. In plot terms, to send Bond to find just a single or cell of suicide bombers or shooters would not make a good film.

Conversely, as in *Spectre*, where the very Secret Service world is a cover for villainy, the villain without can be less important in the Bond corpus than the villain within, notably the Drax figure, who is an establishment figure harboring deadly intentions. In the film *Moonraker*, Drax has played bridge with Britain's Minister of Defence and enjoys taking part in country sports, notably grouse shooting, as well as eating cucumber sandwiches, although Bond tricks Drax in the shooting, thus surviving an attempt to assassinate him.

The choice of villain in *Spectre* is linked both to the modern preference for Britons as villains—every other group claims prejudice if thus depicted—and to the notion of the adventure hero, and particularly spy, as an agent discovering secrets and finding menace as well as combating it. This discovery is different to the challenge posed by an open and self-proclaimed villain. This point, however, raises the question of flexibility. What might have been a coherent style and plot relationship in the past in fact involved changes and developments, as the Bond story shows. How well this might be adapted in the future is unclear.

The debate about the future of Bond concentrated on who might play him and, more generally, whether particular categories of actor might play him. Thus, in the mid-2010s, there was much discussion as to whether a black actor would play Bond, and some discussion over whether a woman could play him. Would, could, and should can overlap. The choice of which word to use says much about the assumptions or supposed assumptions of viewers.

There was far less discussion about the possible direction of the plots. In part, this may reflect the degree of lesser attention devoted to plots compared to the pace of the adventure. Moreover, the series has been able to withstand the popularization of travel and the decline of the exotic and the empire. Nevertheless, the plots are significant, not least because they explain the settings, direct the villain, and structure the script. The plots themselves face the quandary of how to address differing global sensitivities, which, indeed, provide a pointed and commercial aspect of what is more usually discussed as political correctness. Indeed, this is globalization with a vengeance for, in being a global product, the Bond franchise has to face the need to avoid offending part of the market, notably China, where both viewers and financial backing provide a key factor in the economics of the films.

The return of history in the mid-2010s, in response to earlier claims in the 1990s of its "death," provides an instructive context for Bond's future. If history, in the shape of both great power and ideological rivalries, is coming back into prominence, then Bond has an additional role as the defender of the West in this threatening environment. Yet, at the same time, this development creates problems for Bond. If Russia, China, and their allies have become far more hostile to the West, and may become even more hostile, then the problem of Bond as a global force and product will become acute. If relevant to the world, he will not be welcome in such countries. At the same time, Russia and China may produce their own copies; it is through them in part that Bond's influence may become readily apparent. Indeed, the "classic Bond" may in the future be most readily glimpsed in such Bond-like heroes, rather than with a Bond from the politically correct West. A Chinese-made Bond may work better in countries in Asia and Africa that look to China economically.

Again, the present has its revenge in unexpected forms and the future may in even more. The United States of President Trump is a United States that may be much more interested in an American hero, not a British one, not least because the latter seems increasingly politically correct. Again, however, Hollywood may be hesitant about a Trump-like hero, both for American and for global markets, and may prefer Bond. Bond himself will face constraints. It is difficult to see the following in a new Bond novel:

> The villain was not revealed at once. Who could be sabotaging the defense of the West against a sinister foreign dictator? Bond was summoned from his Caribbean retirement beach hut, his winter alternative to the alpine chalet where he kept another lady friend. M was clear about the danger.
>
> "Surely," replied Bond, "I've done this all before. Haven't the Americans learned from my epic adventure in *Diamonds Are Forever* where I thwarted Blofeld after he had taken over the empire of billionaire Willard Whyte by kidnapping and then impersonating him? Which billionaire has Blofeld taken this time?"
>
> "Ah," said M. "It's not that simple. Maybe it is Blofeld, but, at any rate, yet another narcissistic billionaire with a world-mission this time has got himself elected president, and now has the nuclear codes."
>
> "No," said Bond, "this is too fanciful even for that charlatan Fleming."
>
> "Fanciful or not," said M, "you have no choice. You have to save the world."
>
> "Well, at least, this is one that won't be filmed," said Bond, who was totally jaded with the film versions of his life.

Plots and villains are difficult to predict, and part of the joy of the future is its very unpredictability. Given that the Bond persona can be readily applied to any plot (in a way that Bourne cannot), this unpredictability may not be a problem. Indeed, much of the interest for the public is provided by the uncertainty of what the story will be. This matches the situation as far as the successive Le Carré novels and films were concerned, although they faced the difficulties of introducing a new hero in each story, which was not a problem that the Bond scripts faced.

The attraction of a range of models was demonstrated in 2016 by a great television success, that of *The Night Manager*, a version of the 1993 Le Carré novel, but one with many plot changes from the novel. The original novel was a Fleming pastiche, set in the Caribbean. The television series had an immediacy that was closer to the Bourne model, but with a degree of opulence that was closer to the Bond setting, and not least a villainous arms dealer, played by Hugh Laurie, who was a good Bond-type villain, albeit more sophisticated. It is far easier for a Bond film to begin with all engines firing. In contrast, in *The Night Manager*, the hero is drawn into acting as an ally for elements in the British intelligence world and ultimately into killing. He is not an agent like Bond, who can act as an immediate and largely unproblematic action hero. Tom Hiddleston, the actor who played the hero, was at once mentioned as a possible Bond.

Whatever the strengths of the Bond model, competition poses a problem, and this is so whether the future for Bond is a series of present-day battles with evil, or a retro Bond, as in Sebastian Faulks's *Devil May Care* (2008). Retro in practice has its limits, not least with non-Western viewers. Indeed, the topicality of the stories ensures that James Bond is a key guide to the imaginative grasp of danger and espionage in the modern world. The world has proved a threatening and profitable one for Bond, and there is no sign that this will cease.

INDEX